Quick Study

S0-AZP-864

Science

PEARSON
Scott
Foresman

Editorial Offices: Glenview, Illinois • Parsippany, New Jersey • New York, New York
Sales Offices: Needham, Massachusetts • Duluth, Georgia • Glenview, Illinois
Coppell, Texas • Sacramento, California • Mesa, Arizona

www.sfsuccessnet.com

Series Authors

Dr. Timothy Cooney
Professor of Earth Science and Science Education
University of Northern Iowa (UNI)
Cedar Falls, Iowa

Dr. Jim Cummins
Professor
Department of Curriculum, Teaching, and Learning
The University of Toronto
Toronto, Canada

Dr. James Flood
Distinguished Professor of Literacy and Language
School of Teacher Education
San Diego State University
San Diego, California

Barbara Kay Foots, M.Ed.
Science Education Consultant
Houston, Texas

Dr. M. Jenice Goldston
Associate Professor of Science Education
Department of Elementary Education Programs
University of Alabama
Tuscaloosa, Alabama

Dr. Shirley Gholston Key
Associate Professor of Science Education
Instruction and Curriculum Leadership Department
College of Education
University of Memphis
Memphis, Tennessee

Dr. Diane Lapp
Distinguished Professor of Reading and Language Arts in Teacher Education
San Diego State University
San Diego, California

Sheryl A. Mercier
Classroom Teacher
Dunlap Elementary School
Dunlap, California

Dr. Karen L. Ostlund
UTeach, College of Natural Sciences
The University of Texas at Austin
Austin, Texas

Dr. Nancy Romance
Professor of Science Education & Principal Investigator
NSF/IERI Science IDEAS Project
Charles E. Schmidt College of Science
Florida Atlantic University
Boca Raton, Florida

Dr. William Tate
Chair and Professor of Education and Applied Statistics
Department of Education
Washington University
St. Louis, Missouri

Dr. Kathryn C. Thornton
Professor
School of Engineering and Applied Science
University of Virginia
Charlottesville, Virginia

Dr. Leon Ukens
Professor of Science Education
Department of Physics, Astronomy, and Geosciences
Towson University
Towson, Maryland

Steve Weinberg
Consultant
Connecticut Center for Advanced Technology
East Hartford, Connecticut

Consulting Author

Dr. Michael P. Klentschy
Superintendent
El Centro Elementary School District
El Centro, California

ISBN: 0-328-14575-0

Unit A
Life Science

Unit B
Earth Science

Unit C
Physical Science

Unit D
Space and Technology

Lesson 1: What are the main parts of a plant?

Vocabulary

system a set of parts that work together

What All Living Things Need

Most living things need food, air, water, and space to live and grow. Plants and animals have needs. Animals need to eat plants or other animals for food. Plants can make their own food. To make their food, plants need energy from the Sun. Plants also need air, water, and soil. Most plants have four main parts. These parts are leaves, roots, stems, and flowers.

Why Plants Need Leaves

A plant's leaves make up its leaf system. A **system** is made up of parts that work together. Leaves are different shapes and sizes. They make food for plants. The food they make is a kind of sugar.

Leaves use sunlight, carbon dioxide, and water to make food. Carbon dioxide is a gas in the air. Carbon dioxide goes into the leaves through tiny holes in the leaves. Water from the soil enters the plant through the plant's roots and stems.

The leaves change carbon dioxide and water into sugar. The plant uses the sugar to live and grow. When leaves make sugar, they also make a gas. This gas is called oxygen. Oxygen goes out of the plant through the same tiny holes in the leaves.

Other Ways Leaves Help Plants

Leaves help plants get the water they need. Sometimes plants get too much water. When this happens, the plant lets some water out through the tiny holes in its leaves. Some plants that live in dry places have leaves covered with wax or fuzz. This helps the plant keep the water in.

Some plants have leaves that are poisonous, sharp, or tough to chew. This helps protect the plants from bugs or animals that might eat it.

Lesson 1 Checkpoint

1. What do plants and animals need to live?

_____

_____

2. List the main parts of most plants.

_____

_____

3. How does a leaf help a plant live?

_____

_____

_____

_____

4. **Compare and Contrast** Describe ways that leaves are alike and different. Use a graphic organizer.

Lesson 2: Why do plants need roots and stems?

How Roots Help Plants

A plant's root system is usually below the ground. We cannot see a plant's roots. The roots hold the plant in the ground. Roots take in water and minerals from the soil. Minerals are materials in the soil. They help plants grow. Roots also store food that plants make.

Different plants have different kinds of roots. Some plants have one large root that grows deep in the soil. This is called a taproot. Carrots and dandelions have taproots.

Tiny root hairs grow from the tips of roots. They help the plant take in water and minerals. The root hairs grow far into the soil to reach water. Water goes through tubes to the plant's stem and leaves.

On hot days, the sun and hot air can dry out a plant. The plant loses water through its leaves. The root system must take in enough water to replace the water it loses.

How Stems Help Plants

A plant's stems hold up its leaves, flowers, and fruits. Tubes in the plant stems move water and minerals from the roots to the leaves. These tubes also move food from the leaves to the stems and roots.

Different plants have different kinds of stems. Some stems are thin. They grow along the ground. These stems can grow roots and a new plant. Some stems grow and wrap around poles that hold up the plant.

Cactus stems can be very fat. Cactus stems store water. They get fatter as they store more water. They get thinner as the plant uses the water. Cactus stems have a thick, waxy covering. This helps the cactus plant keep in water and live in a desert.

Like roots, parts of some stems grow under the ground. A potato is part of the stem of the potato plant. It gets fatter as it stores food. Underground stems can grow new stems. These stems grow from buds. The bud of a potato is called an "eye." The underground stems grow up through the soil. They become new potato plants.

Some stems have thorns or hairs that sting. This helps protect the stem from hungry animals that might eat it.

Lesson 2 Checkpoint

1. How do roots help a plant?

_____

_____

2. How do stems help a plant?

_____

_____

_____

_____

3. How are roots and stems alike and different?

_____

_____

_____

_____

Lesson 3: How are plants grouped?

Vocabulary

deciduous loses its leaves in the fall and grows new ones in the spring

pollinate move pollen from the part of a flower that makes pollen to the part of a flower that makes seeds

coniferous does not lose its needle-like leaves in the fall

Flowering Plants

Trees and herbs are both plants. But trees and herbs are in different groups. Plants in each group have different kinds of roots, stems, leaves, and flowers. Trees have stiff, woody stems to help hold them up. They can grow very large. The stems of herbs do not have wood. They grow close to the ground. In the fall, many herbs die. Only the roots stay alive. In the spring, herbs grow a new stem and leaves. But on trees, only the leaves die and fall off in the fall. The tree grows new leaves in the spring. Trees that lose their leaves are **deciduous.**

Making Seeds

Flowers make seeds. Flowers have petals. Flowers also have parts that make pollen or seeds. Bees and other animals **pollinate** a flower. They move pollen to the flower part that makes seeds. The wind can also pollinate a flower.

After bees pollinate the flower, seeds form near the center of the flower. A fruit grows around the seeds to protect them.

Coniferous Trees

Coniferous trees do not lose their leaves in the fall. They have cones instead of flowers. The cones make seeds. The leaves of coniferous trees look like needles or brushes. Some coniferous trees are pine, fir, spruce, and hemlock.

Two Types of Cones

Pine cones come from coniferous trees. Coniferous trees make two kinds of pine cones. They make big and small cones. The small cones make pollen. The big cones make seeds. Wind blows pollen from the small pollen cones to the large seed cones. When pollen attaches to the seed cone, a seed begins to grow.

Seeds grow inside the seed cones. When the seeds are ripe, they fall to the ground. If the temperature, soil, and water are good for the seeds, they can begin to grow. They may grow into trees.

Lesson 3 Checkpoint

1. Describe how a flower makes a seed.

_____

_____

_____

_____

2. What are two ways to group plants?

_____

_____

3. Describe two kinds of plant parts that can make seeds.

_____

_____

_____

_____

Lesson 4: How do new plants grow?

Vocabulary

seed leaf part of a seed that has stored food

germinate begin to grow

seedling a new, small plant that grows from a seed

Scattering Seeds

Seeds are spread or scattered in different ways. Wind or water can move seeds from one place to another. Animals eat fruit with seeds. Then the animals carry the seeds to new places. The seeds move through the animal's body and drop to the ground. Some seeds stick to the fur of an animal or to a person's clothing. Seeds often move far away from the plant they came from.

Wind carries seeds that are very light. Many seeds have special parts that help them float far away. The seeds can go a long way if the wind is strong.

Special Ways of Releasing Seeds

Some kinds of pine cones need to be heated to drop their seeds. Forest fires heat cones so they drop seeds. Forest fires also remove plants around the trees. This makes space for the seeds to grow.

Germinating and Growing

Seeds come in different sizes, shapes, and colors. But all seeds have the same parts. All seeds can grow into new plants.

Every seed has a seed coat to protect the inside of the seed. There is a tiny new plant inside each seed. All seeds have a **seed leaf.** The plant uses food in the seed leaf to help it grow.

Seeds need certain things to **germinate,** or begin to grow. They need the right temperature, the right amount of water, and air. If a seed has these things, it begins to sprout. The seed breaks open and a young plant begins to grow. This small plant is a **seedling.** The seedling grows and comes out of the soil. Then the seedling grows leaves. The leaves use sunlight to make sugar for food. The seedling grows into an adult plant with flowers. The flowers are pollinated. They make new seeds. Then the seeds grow into new plants. This is the plant's life cycle.

Lesson 4 Checkpoint

1. What are two ways that animals scatter seeds?

_____

_____

2. What are the parts of a seed?

_____

3. Describe the life cycle of a plant starting with a seed being planted.

_____

_____

_____

_____

Lesson 5: How are plants from the past like today's plants?

Vocabulary

fossil the remains or marks of a living thing from long ago

extinct no longer lives on Earth

Plants That Lived Long Ago

We study fossils to learn about plants that lived long ago. A **fossil** is the remains or mark of a living thing from long ago. A plant fossil is a mark made by a plant. The plant part died and was pressed into mud. An outline of the plant was made in the mud. The mud got hard. Over time the mud turned into rock.

Petrified wood is wood that turns into stone. This takes a very long time. Petrified wood starts to form when a tree falls into a river. In the river, the tree gets filled with water. The tree gets buried in mud. Over time, minerals fill in tiny spaces in the wood of the trees. After a very long time, the wood turns into stone. The stone has exactly the same shape as the original wood.

Many kinds of plants that lived long ago are no longer alive today. They are **extinct.** For example, ferns today look different from the ferns that lived long ago.

Plants Change Over Time

Plant fossils show us that the first plants did not have flowers or cones. Many of the first plants were like ferns and horsetails.

The Earth changed over time. The plants changed too. Trees with pine cones began to grow. Then plants with flowers grew. Many of the first plants have disappeared. They do not grow on Earth today.

Magnolias were one of the first plants with flowers. They have survived from long ago. When magnolias first grew, the world was warm and wet all year. Dinosaurs were everywhere. Magnolias grew thick leaves. They had leaves all year. Over many years, magnolias changed. Today, some magnolias are deciduous. This means they lose their leaves in the fall. But their leaves and flowers look similar to magnolias that lived many years ago. The magnolia flower has not changed for 100 million years.

Lesson 5 Checkpoint

1. What can scientists learn by studying fossils?

_____

_____

2. What is an extinct plant?

_____

_____

3. How do scientists learn about plants that are extinct?

_____

_____

4. ⊙ **Compare and Contrast** How are extinct magnolias alike and different from magnolias alive today? Use a graphic organizer to show your answer.

Use with pp. 39–43

Lesson 1: How are animals grouped?

Vocabulary

> **trait** a body feature passed onto an animal from its parents
>
> **vertebrate** animal with a backbone

What All Animals Need

All animals need food, water, oxygen, and shelter to live. Animals can drink water or get water from the foods they eat. All animals need oxygen, which is a gas in the air. Most animals that live on land have lungs to breathe in oxygen. Many animals that live in water have gills to breathe in oxygen. Animals eat plants or other animals for food. Shelters protect animals from the weather and other animals. Some animals build shelters. Others have their own hard shells as homes and to protect them.

Ways of Grouping Animals

Sometimes we group animals by where they live or how they act. We can also group animals by how they look. A **trait** is a body feature that is passed onto an animal from its parents. Traits can also be things an animal does.

An animal might be placed in more than one group. For example, we can group animals by what they eat. Snakes, hawks, and owls eat mice. Hawks and owls are also in a group of animals that can fly.

Animals With Backbones

An animal with a backbone is called a **vertebrate.** Cats, dogs, and birds are vertebrates. Fish and snakes are vertebrates too. Vertebrate animals can look different, but they all have backbones.

There are five groups of vertebrates. Fish, amphibians, reptiles, birds, and mammals are the five kinds of vertebrates. Fish spend their lives in water. Most fish have scales and breathe through gills. Frogs and toads are amphibians. Many amphibians spend part of their lives in water and part on land. Most young amphibians live in water and get their oxygen through their moist skin and gills. As they grow, most amphibians develop lungs to breathe.

Reptiles usually have dry, scaly skin. They have lungs to breathe air. Snakes, lizards, and turtles are reptiles.

Birds have bills and feathers. They do not have teeth. Birds breathe air through lungs. Wings and light bones help birds fly. Feathers help keep birds warm.

Most mammals have hair to keep them warm. Mammals breathe air through lungs and feed milk to their babies.

Animals Without Backbones

Most animals do not have skeletons made of bone inside their bodies. These animals are called invertebrates. Sea jellies, worms, mollusks, and arthropods are the major kinds of invertebrate animals. Many mollusks have a soft body inside a hard outside shell. Octopus, clams, and snails are mollusks. Arthropods are the largest group of animals without backbones. Arthropods wear their skeletons outside their bodies. They have legs with joints. Spiders and crabs are arthropods.

Shells and skeletons outside the body would weigh too much on big animals. So animals without backbones cannot grow as large as vertebrates.

Most sea jellies live in the ocean, while worms live in the soil. A small area of soil can have several million roundworms. There are more animals without backbones than animals with backbones.

© Pearson Education, Inc. 3

Quick Study

Lesson 1 Checkpoint

1. What do all animals need?

_____

_____

2. Should reptiles and amphibians be grouped together? Explain your answer.

_____

_____

_____

_____

3. If a rattlesnake and a black widow spider both make poison, why are they put in different groups?

_____

_____

_____

_____

4. Explain why most invertebrates are small in size compared to most vertebrates.

_____

_____

Lesson 2: How do animals grow and change?

Vocabulary

larva stage in an insect's life after it hatches from the egg

pupa stage in insect's life after larva, when it is in a hard covering

Life Cycles

An animal's life starts out as an egg. Sometimes the egg develops inside the mother who gives birth to a live baby. For other animals, the mother lays an egg outside her body. The young animal develops in the egg and hatches when it is ready. Some baby animals look like their parents when they hatch or are born. But most animals have to grow before they look like their parents. The stages of the life cycle are birth, growth, development, reproduction, and death.

A Butterfly's Life Cycle

The butterfly's life cycle begins in an egg. The egg is so tiny it is hard to see.

Next a caterpillar hatches from the egg. The caterpillar is now a **larva.** The caterpillar must eat a lot to survive.

As it grows, the caterpillar sheds its skin and forms a hard cover around itself. This cover is called a chrysalis. The larva's body changes inside the chrysalis. The larva is now a **pupa.** Its body changes a lot while it is a pupa. It grows wings and legs with joints. It begins to look like an adult butterfly.

It breaks the chrysalis and crawls out. The adult butterfly dries its wings and flies away to look for a mate. The butterfly finds a mate and lays eggs. Finally its life cycle ends when it dies.

Some Vertebrate Life Cycles

The life cycles of vertebrates can be very different. Some vertebrates, such as frogs change many times as they grow. Other vertebrates, such as pandas or monkeys, do not change much as they grow.

A Frog's Life Cycle

Amphibians change very much as they become adults. Did you know that a frog acts more like a fish when it is very young?

The frog completes all the stages of its life cycle in one summer. Frogs grow in different ways. In colder places, frogs dig into the mud during the winter and will not become adult frogs until the spring or summer.

The adult frog lays eggs in the water. Tadpoles hatch from the frog eggs. Tadpoles grow and live underwater. They use gills to breathe. Then the tadpole grows and changes. Its tail gets shorter. Its legs start to grow. The back legs grow first. It grows lungs so that it can breathe air on land. Finally it becomes an adult frog that lives on land. It goes back to the water to lay eggs.

A Mammal's Life Cycle

Mammals do not change a lot as they grow. Many mammals look like their parents when they are born. Mammals grow as they get older. Most mammals develop inside their mother's body. When they are born, they are given milk from their mother. They also have hair or fur.

Humans take a long time to become adults. But some mammals become adults in only a few weeks. For example, a baby rabbit leaves the nest when it is less than three weeks old. It will be an adult at six months.

Quick Study

Lesson 2 Checkpoint

1. What is the purpose of the pupa?

_____

2. 🔘 **Sequence** List the sequence of steps in a butterfly's life cycle.
Use the signal words *first, next, then,* and *finally.*

_____

_____

_____

_____

3. Before a frog can live on land, how must its body change?

_____

_____

4. How is a mammal's life cycle different from a frog's or butterfly's life
cycle?

_____

_____

_____

_____

Lesson 3: How do adaptations help animals?

Vocabulary

adaptation trait that helps an animal meet its needs in the place it lives

inherited adaptations passed on from parent to offspring

migrate move to another place when the seasons change

hibernate during cold winter months, to slow down body systems to save energy

Adaptations

A trait that helps an animal meet its needs in the place it lives is an **adaptation.** The webbed feet of a pelican are an adaptation. They help the pelican swim and survive in the water. Adaptations are **inherited,** or passed on, from parents to their young. Body parts such as feet and bills are important inherited adaptations. Most animals have many adaptations to help them live.

Adaptations for Getting Food

Animals have many special adaptations for getting food. Prairie dogs and moles have feet that are good for digging. Hawks and eagles have feet that can hold tightly on to their food. Animals may have special teeth to help them eat. Many birds have bills to help catch and eat their food.

Adaptations for Protection

The way an animal looks and acts can help it survive. Some animals protect themselves by looking dangerous. Other animals blend into the area around them so they are hard to see. Many animals climb, run, hop, jump, fly, or swim away from danger.

Some animals use poison to protect themselves. Skunks and weasels spray a bad odor at their enemies. Special body parts like shells, teeth, claws, hooves, beaks, or pointed body parts can protect animals from danger.

The porcupine is covered in quills. The porcupine uses muscles to make the quills stand up when it is scared. Then it turns around and raises its tail. The porcupine's

quills can cut into an attacker's skin. The hooks on the quills keep them attached to the attacker.

Behaviors That Help Animals

Behaviors are things that you do. Many behaviors are inherited. For example, walking and talking are inherited behaviors. Reading and writing are not inherited behaviors. You have to learn how to read and write. But your ability to learn these behaviors is inherited.

Instincts

An instinct is a behavior that an animal can do when it is born. One instinct is to respond to hunger. Baby birds open their mouths when they sense a parent with food is near. Some animals have an instinct to move, or **migrate,** when the seasons change. Butterflies migrate thousands of miles in the winter. This helps them survive the winter. Other animals have an instinct to **hibernate** in the winter. An animal's body system slows down when it hibernates to save energy.

Learning

Animals learn some behaviors from their parents and other animals. Chimpanzees can learn how to use tools to catch insects. They don't know how to use tools when they are born. They learn how to use tools by watching other chimpanzees. Young chimpanzees watch what their parents and other adults eat. This is how they learn which foods are safe to eat.

Lesson 3 Checkpoint

1. Give two examples of adaptations and tell how they help the animal survive.

   _____

   _____

2. What are some ways that animals protect themselves from their enemies?

   _____

   _____

3. **Sequence** List in the correct sequence what happens when a predator attacks a porcupine. Be sure to use the signal words *first, next,* and *finally* in your list of steps.

   _____

   _____

   _____

   _____

4. Name two types of adaptations having to do with an animal's actions.

   _____

   _____

5. Why do some animals migrate or hibernate?

   _____

   _____

Lesson 4: How are animals from the past like today's animals?

Animals That Lived Long Ago

Fossils are signs of past life. Usually, only the hard parts of animals become fossils. A fossil is usually not the actual bone, but a rock in the shape of the bone.

After an animal dies, its remains become covered with soft earth. The remains wear away. This leaves a mold, or space, in the earth. Over time, the mold fills with rock. The rock has the shape of the animal. This is called a fossil mold.

Ancient Insects

Small animals or parts of animals have been found in amber. Amber is hardened tree sap. Long ago, an insect got trapped in the sticky sap. Soon the sap covered the insect. In time, the sap turned into the hard yellow or reddish-brown substance called amber. You can see the animal's body covering through the amber. It is millions of years old.

We find another type of fossil in tar pits. Thousands of years ago, saber-toothed tigers and other extinct animals fell into these oily pools. The soft parts of their bodies broke down. Only the bones remained. These fossils are the actual bones of these animals.

How Animals Today Compare to Those of Long Ago

Fossils can tell us how animals have changed over time. Dinosaurs are extinct. An extinct animal no longer lives on Earth. But some animals today look like animals of long ago.

Fossils also tell us how Earth has changed over time. The drawing on pages 56–57 of your textbook shows the Badlands of South Dakota more than 65 million years ago. At that time, dinosaurs like *Tyrannosaurus Rex* lived there. Plant fossils were found in this area. These plant fossils show that the climate was hot and wet. That is why you see plants in the drawing of the *T. rex*.

Over time, the place where the *T. rex* lived became hot and dry. The picture on pages 56–57 also shows what the Badlands look like today. The Badlands are almost like a desert. Only animals that can live in hot, dry conditions live there now.

Lesson 4 Checkpoint

1. What are some ways that fossils form?

_____

_____

_____

_____

2. Describe four kinds of fossils.

_____

_____

_____

_____

3. What can fossils tell us about extinct animals?

_____

_____

Lesson 1: What are ecosystems?

Vocabulary

environment everything that surrounds a living thing

ecosystem all the living and nonliving things that interact with each other in a given area

population all the living things of the same kind that live in the same place at the same time

community all the populations that live together in the same place

Places for Living Things

Each living thing needs a certain **environment.** An environment has living and nonliving parts. Plants, animals, and other living things are the living parts. The nonliving parts are the Sun's rays, air, water, and soil.

We need the Sun's rays to live. The Sun's rays make the air, water, and soil warm so we can live. Sunlight shines on the leaves of plants. Plants need sunlight to make food.

Climate shapes each environment. Climate is the weather in a place all through the year. For example, a place may have cold, wet winters and hot, dry summers.

Water and soil are important parts of each environment. Rain and snow fall. Water goes into the soil. Each plant type needs a certain amount of water and a certain kind of soil.

Parts of an Ecosystem

The living and nonliving parts of an environment work together. These parts make up an **ecosystem.** The living parts of an ecosystem need the nonliving parts to live. For example, coastal redwood trees need sunlight, soil, and air. They also need a lot of water.

The living parts of an ecosystem also depend on one another. For example, some sea birds get fish from the ocean. Then they fly to land. They build their nests in the redwood trees.

Special Homes

A habitat is where a living thing makes its home. It has everything that a plant or animal needs to live. It gives plants light, air, water, and a space to live. It also gives them insects that pollinate the plants. The habitat gives animals food, water, shelter, and a space to live. If any of these things are missing, the plants or animals may die or move to a new habitat.

Groups Within Ecosystems

Coyotes live together in groups. A group of living things that are the same and live together is called a **population.** Coyotes hunt squirrels. A **community** is all the populations that live together in the same place. The coyotes, squirrels, and their habitat make up a community. The populations in a community need each other for food and shelter.

Ecosystems Change

Ecosystems usually change over time. The change starts when one part of the ecosystem changes. For example, a habitat may get more rain than usual. Plants will grow more. Ground squirrels will have more food. So the population of ground squirrels will grow.

The coyotes eat squirrels. So the coyotes will have plenty of food. The population of squirrels will go down.

If there is less rain than usual, fewer plants will grow. There will be fewer squirrels. The coyote population will stay small or decrease.

Lesson 1 Checkpoint

1. Name four nonliving things that are part of a plant's or animal's environment.

_____

_____

2. What is an ecosystem?

_____

_____

3. **Main Idea and Details** Read the caption about dune grass on page 73 of your textbook. Give the main idea. List details supporting it.

_____

_____

_____

4. How do coyotes, ground squirrels, and plants interact in their environment?

_____

_____

_____

_____

5. What might happen to plants and animals if there is more rain than usual?

_____

_____

_____

_____

Lesson 2: Which ecosystems have few trees?

Vocabulary

grassland ecosystem that has many grasses and few trees

desert ecosystem that gets very little rain and has high daytime temperatures

tundra land ecosystem that is the coldest and farthest north

Grassland

A **grassland** is a kind of land ecosystem. It has many grasses and flowering plants. It does not have many trees. Grasslands have cold winters and hot summers. The climate includes little rain, so the soil is dry. Trees cannot grow in dry soil. They need water to grow. The trees grow mostly in the wetter soil along rivers and creeks.

Many grasses grow well in this kind of habitat. They have deep roots that help them survive. There are many ways that deep roots help the plants. When grazing animals, fire, or the cold winters kill the plants above ground the roots survive. Deep roots help plants find this water when there is no new rain water in the summer.

Desert—A Surprising Ecosystem

A **desert** is another kind of ecosystem. A desert gets very little rain. Days are hot. Nights are cool or cold. Many people think that deserts only have sand. But most desert ecosystems have plants and animals. Desert plants and animals can live with very little rain water. Certain plants, like cactuses, store water in their stems.

During the day, you might see a lizard sitting in the sun. But many desert animals rest where you cannot see them. Some stay in underground tunnels. Others stay in the shade under a plant. At night, the desert animals come out. They look for food.

Tundra—Land of Long Winters

The **tundra** is another kind of land ecosystem. The tundra is cold and dry. It is in the very northern part of the world. Parts of Alaska are tundra. Winters are long and cold. Summers are short and cool. The snow melts in summer, but the soil stays hard. The soil stays frozen all year around.

In the tundra, summer days are very long. In some places, the Sun shines 24 hours a day. Winter days are very short. Some places get no sunlight at all in the winter.

Many plants cannot grow in this climate. For example, there are no trees in the tundra. Their roots cannot grow in the frozen soil. Only small plants can grow. These include grasses and wildflowers.

In summer, the snow melts. The water makes ponds. Many ducks, geese, and swans live near the ponds. Other birds make nests in the tundra. In the summer, there are millions of insects for the birds to eat. Most tundra birds go to warmer places in the winter.

© Pearson Education, Inc. 3

Lesson 2 Checkpoint

1. What is a grassland?

_____

_____

2. **Main Idea and Details** Tell the main idea about grasslands.
Give supporting details.

_____

_____

_____

_____

3. Why do certain plants do well in deserts?

_____

_____

4. What is the coldest land ecosystem?

_____

5. List three kinds of land ecosystems.

_____

_____

_____

Lesson 3: What are some forest ecosystems?

Coniferous and Deciduous Forests

Coniferous forests grow in the northern areas of North America, Europe, and Asia. They grow in places where the winters are cold and snowy. They grow in places where the summers are warm and dry. These forests have many coniferous trees, such as spruce, fir, and pine. Their leaves look like needles. These needles do not break when a lot of snow falls on them.

Many birds live in coniferous forests. They can find food and shelter. Birds and squirrels eat seeds from the cones of these trees. Deer and moose eat plants that grow near lakes and streams. Wolves hunt other animals.

Deciduous forests grow in some of the same places that conifers grow. Deciduous forests grow in warmer climates than coniferous forests. Deciduous forests get rain in summer and snow in winter.

Oaks, maples, and beech trees grow in deciduous forests. These trees drop their leaves in fall. For part of the year sunlight reaches the forest floor. Many shrubs and plants can grow there. Animals eat the plants. Many insects, birds, and small animals live in deciduous forests.

Tropical Forests

Tropical forests grow near the equator. The climate in a tropical forest is warm and rainy all year long. The tropical forest has a lot of tall trees. Some of the trees can be 35 meters tall. That is taller than a ten-story office building. The tall trees block the sunlight. So the forest floor gets very little sunlight. Plants such as orchids grow on the trees.

Most animals in the tropical forest live in the trees. Some spend their whole lives there. Some of these animals are bats, monkeys, birds, and many insects. The tropical rainforest has huge numbers of insects. No one has ever named them all.

Lesson 3 Checkpoint

1. How are coniferous and deciduous forests alike and different?

_____

_____

2. What kind of climate can tropical forests have?

_____

_____

3. List three kinds of forests.

_____

_____

_____

Lesson 4: What are water ecosystems?

Vocabulary

wetland low land ecosystem that is covered by water at least part of the time during the year

Freshwater Ecosystems

Freshwater ecosystems include lakes, ponds, rivers, and streams. Lakes and ponds are water with land around them. Rivers and streams are moving water. Most lakes or rivers get water from rain or melting snow. Springs that flow underground supply water for others. Many plants and animals live in lakes and rivers.

The Everglades is in south Florida. It is a large wetland. A **wetland** is low land that is covered by water at least part of the year. The water in the Everglades is not deep. It is very shallow. Trees, grasses, and water plants live there. Animals like fish, bears, and birds live there too.

Saltwater Ecosystems

Oceans cover a lot of the Earth's surface. Ocean water has salt. The ocean is shallow near land. Clams, crabs, algae, fish, and coral live close to the shore. Otters, seals, and sea birds swim and dive for fish.

The ocean water gets deeper farther from land. Most life is in the top 200 meters of the deep water. Fish, shrimp, and whales live there. The deep ocean is dark and cold. It does not have much food. Few animals live there.

Many rivers flow into the ocean. Fresh water from the river mixes with salt water from the ocean. Salt marshes can form. Salt marshes are wetlands that have special plants and animals.

The organisms that live in salt marshes can live in salty water and soil. Many plants grow in salt marshes. Many tiny living animals live in salt marshes too. Some are too small to see with just your eyes. Many kinds of fish, crabs, and other ocean animals are born in the salt marshes.

Quick Study

Lesson 4 Checkpoint

1. Name four kinds of freshwater ecosystems.

_____

_____

2. Where do most corals live?

_____

_____

3. Where is most life found in the oceans?

_____

_____

Lesson 1: How do living things interact?

Ways Living Things Interact

Living things in the same environment interact with each other in different ways. This helps them to survive.

Some living things live in groups. The members of a group help each other. Sometimes one living thing helps another kind of living thing. For example, a large tree can be a home for a small plant. Other living things help each other. Insects and flowers help each other. The insects get food from the plants. The flowers get pollen.

Living in Groups

Animals that live together may share jobs. Some animals help protect their group from other animals that want to hurt them. Animals are safer in a group than when they are alone.

Prairie dogs live in groups. Coyotes and eagles eat prairie dogs. Coyotes hunt on the ground. Eagles hunt from the air. Prairie dogs take turns to watch the opening of their burrows. The prairie dog whistles if it sees danger. The group hears the whistle. They all run and hide until it is safe to come out.

One Kind of Living Thing Helping Another

Different kinds of living things interact with each other in different ways.

A barnacle is an animal in the ocean. Some barnacles try to stick onto the skin of a whale. Many barnacles can live on one whale. The whale moves through the water. The barnacle opens and closes its shell to catch food in the water. The barnacles do not hurt the whales. The barnacles do not help the whales either. But the whales help the barnacles move and get food.

Helping One Another

Sometimes living things help each other. A special moth helps the yucca plant. The moth gives it pollen from another yucca plant. The plant helps the moth. It gives it a place to live. It also gives it food for its young. The moth lays eggs in the yucca plant.

Some fish also help each other. Some small fish eat the things that live on bigger fish. The small fish get food from the bigger fish. The bigger fish get clean and stay healthy.

Lesson 1 Checkpoint

1. List three ways in which living things might interact.

_____

_____

_____

_____

2. Give two examples of how living things benefit from living together.

_____

_____

_____

3. How do yucca moths and yucca plants help each other?

_____

_____

_____

4. **Draw Conclusions** Why do living things interact?

_____

_____

_____

Lesson 2: How do living things get energy?

Vocabulary

producer a living thing that makes its own food

consumer a living thing that eats food

herbivore a consumer that eats only plants

carnivore a consumer that eats only animals

omnivore a consumer that eats both plants and animals

prey an animal that is hunted by others for food

predator a consumer that hunts for food

Sources of Energy

Green plants make their own food. Living things that make their own food are producers. **Producers** use energy from the Sun to make food. Producers also need air and soil to make food.

Many living things cannot make their own food. They must get their energy from food they eat. They are **consumers.**

Kinds of Consumers

There are three kinds of consumers. **Herbivores** are consumers that eat only plants. Cows and grasshoppers are herbivores. **Carnivores** are consumers that hunt other animals for food. Wolves and badgers are carnivores. **Omnivores** are consumers that eat both plants and animals. People and bears are omnivores.

Food Chains

Food chains and food webs are groups of producers and consumers. Energy in a food chain moves from one living thing to another.

One food chain starts with a cattail plant. The cattail uses energy from the Sun to make its food. A crayfish eats the cattail. The cattail transfers its energy to the crayfish. Then a raccoon eats the crayfish. The raccoon gets energy from the crayfish.

The energy moves from the cattail to the crayfish to the raccoon.

In this food chain, the cattail is a producer. The crayfish and the raccoon are consumers. The crayfish is prey. **Prey** is an animal that is hunted by others for food. The prey gives energy to the predator. A **predator** is a consumer that hunts for food. The raccoon is a predator.

A food web is made up of more than one food chain. Energy might transfer from one kind of producer to many kinds of consumers. One kind of consumer might be prey for more than one kind of predator.

A Changing Food Web

When one part of a food chain or food web is lost, the other parts change too. For example, prairie dogs and cows eat the same grasses. Sometimes ranchers kill the prairie dogs so cows can have more food.

But the prairie dogs are also prey. Ferrets eat prairie dogs. Reducing the number of prairie dogs means ferrets have less food. They do not get energy they need. Many die.

Badgers eat ferrets. When many ferrets die, the badgers have to look for other food. The loss of prairie dogs also hurts other animals. Golden eagles and foxes also eat prairie dogs. Now they need to get their food energy from other animals.

© Pearson Education, Inc. 3

Lesson 2 Checkpoint

1. Trace the transfer of energy through a food chain that includes raccoons, crayfish, cattails, and sunlight.

_____

_____

_____

2. How did reducing the number of prairie dogs affect ferrets?

_____

_____

3. How does the loss of prairie dogs affect eagles and foxes?

_____

_____

4. **Draw Conclusions** Tell what happens when a food chain is broken.

_____

_____

Lesson 3: How do living things compete?

Vocabulary

competition when two or more living things need the same resource

Competing for Resources

A forest is dark and cool. It has a lot of tall trees. It has only a few small trees. The tall trees block the sun. The small trees are in competition with one another for sunlight. Living things are in **competition** when they need the same resource. The tall trees get most of the sunlight. It is hard for the small trees to survive.

Living things compete for light, food, water, living space, and other resources. Some living things also compete for mates. The winners of these competitions survive. The losers may not survive.

Predators and Prey

Members of predator populations may compete for prey. Predators that are fast and strong catch more food. Some birds steal prey from other birds. Predators that can get more food will survive and have young. The young may be fast and strong like their parents.

Different kinds of predators also compete for prey. Lions and hyenas may want the same prey. Lions hunt and kill the prey. Hyenas fight the lions. Hyenas try to steal the prey from the lions.

Prey animals also compete with each other. Deer that are strong and healthy are more likely to survive. It is easier for them to find mates and to get away from predators.

Different Kinds of Competition

Sometimes, living things compete for space. Loosestrife is a purple plant. Someone brought it into the United States a long time ago. It grows well near rivers. Animals do not eat it, so it keeps growing. Now purple loosestrife takes space away from other plants. It is winning the competition for space in many places.

Sometimes animals and people compete for space. People move to places where animals live. They see coyotes in their backyards. They find sea gulls on their beaches.

Living things also compete for oxygen. Algae are tiny plants. They give food and oxygen to fish and other animals. When there are too many algae at the surface, some of the algae in the water do not get the light they need. They die. Living things that eat the dead algae use up a lot of oxygen in the pond. Fish and frogs compete for the oxygen that is left in the pond.

Sometimes competition follows a cycle. A cycle is a group of events that repeats.

For example, lemmings are small mammals. They eat grass, seeds, and roots. The lemming population has a cycle of change. About every three years their population grows large. Then the lemmings use up many of their resources. Now the lemmings have to compete for what they need. Some lemmings cannot find enough resources to live. Many of them leave. They look for new habitats. Now there are fewer lemmings. There is less competition for food. The grasses grow back. The cycle begins again. The lemming population begins to grow.

Lesson 3 Checkpoint

1. What do living things compete for?

_____

_____

2. Why do living things compete with one another?

_____

_____

3. What kind of living thing usually survives in a competition?

_____

_____

4. **Draw Conclusions** Explain the pattern of change in the lemming population over time.

_____

_____

_____

Lesson 4: How do environments change?

Vocabulary

decomposer a living thing that breaks down waste and things that
have died

decay the action of breaking down waste and things that have died

Causes of Change

Animals can change the environment.
Beavers build dams. Water fills the area. A
new wetland habitat grows. Fish, birds, and
other animals can live there. The dams flood
places that used to be dry. Animals that lived
on the dry land have to look for new homes.

Natural events can also change ecosystems.
Hurricanes can change coastlines. They can
knock down trees and wear away sand. They
can cause floods. Floods kill plants. They wash
away birds' nests. They spread mud all over.
Floods move soil from one place to another.

A drought is another kind of natural event.
It is very dry during a drought. Little rain falls.
Plants cannot get the water they need. So
plants die. It is hard for many animals to find
water during a drought. Some animals die.
Other animals have to move to new places.

Living Things Return

In 1980, a huge volcano in Washington
called Mt. St. Helens erupted. This changed the
environment. It burned trees and destroyed
forests. Mud and rocks covered large areas.
In some places, the ash was three feet thick.
Few things lived after the eruption. Then wind
blew seeds of grass, flowers, and trees to the
mountain. Plants began to grow again.

Spiders, beetles, and birds went back to
live on Mt. St. Helens. Each year, more plants
grew. More animals went back to eat the
plants. Now, squirrels, deer, and elk live there.

Fires also change environments. Lightning
may hit a tree. The tree burns. The fire then
burns plants on the forest floor. But the plants
that do not burn now have more space. Also,
the ash from fires helps plants to grow.

Eruptions and fires are examples of events
that change environments. The changes often
kill plants. They can destroy animal homes.
But the changes may also make new habitats
for other plants and animals.

Patterns of Change

Living things change together. The changes
happen in patterns. Douglas fir and western
hemlock are two types of trees. They grow
in the same forests. Their life cycles are
connected.

Douglas fir trees have cones. Squirrels knock
the cones to the ground. Seeds in the cones
sprout on the forest floor. They compete for
light and other resources. A few survive. They
grow into giant trees. Some grow old and die.

Mushrooms and other **decomposers** work
on the dead trees. A decomposer is a living
thing that breaks down wastes and things
that have died. This is called **decay.** Trees use
materials in the soil to help them grow. Decay
gives some of these materials back to the soil.
When trees die, decomposers help them break
down into the soil.

Seeds from the hemlock cones fall on the
decaying Douglas fir logs. The logs hold water
better than the ground. The logs contain
things young hemlock seedlings need to grow.
Also, now there is sunlight in the forest where
the big trees used to be. The hemlocks grow
quickly. They become tall trees. The trees are
homes for squirrels, owls, and other animals.
Carpenter ants come after the trees die. They
make nests in the tree trunks. The trees fall to
the ground. They decay and become part of
the soil. The life cycles of many living things
are connected.

© Pearson Education, Inc. 3

Lesson 4 Checkpoint

1. Describe ways that living things and natural events can cause an environment to change.

   _____

   _____

2. Explain how fire is a change that can improve growing conditions for plants.

   _____

   _____

   _____

3. List natural events that can cause change in an environment.

   _____

   _____

4. Describe patterns of change involving Douglas fir and western hemlock trees.

   _____

   _____

   _____

   _____

Lesson 5: What is a healthy environment for people?

What People Need

People need food to survive. Food comes from farms and ranches. People buy it at the store.

People also need clean water to drink. They need clean air to breathe. They need shelter. Shelter keeps people safe from the weather. It also keeps them at a good temperature.

People need a clean environment. They must remove waste to keep the environment clean. Garbage and other wastes go to different places. Some communities put garbage in a landfill.

Water

In some countries, people get water from streams. Most water in the United States comes from wells. Water also comes from special lakes called reservoirs.

Food

Our food may come from far away. Fresh food may arrive on airplanes, boats, and trucks. Other foods may be canned or frozen.

Shelter

Shelter is different in different places. People in hot climates need cool places to live. In cold climates, they need warm places. People in cities often live in big buildings.

Air

There are less people in open spaces than in cities. There are not as many cars and factories. The air is cleaner in open spaces.

Clean Environment

Everyone can help protect the environment. A healthy environment helps people stay healthy.

Healthful Foods

People need a variety of foods to be healthy. Different foods give us all the vitamins, minerals, and other nutrients our bodies need.

People need whole grains, fruits, and vegetables. They also eat nuts, fish, eggs, dairy foods, and meats. They need a good amount of water as well.

Food should be stored carefully. This keeps it clean and healthful. Fresh fruits and vegetables should be washed and kept cool. Fish, eggs, dairy foods, and meats should be kept cool. Food should be wrapped and cooked soon. Food that is stored too long loses nutrients.

Cooks must wash their hands before they touch food. They must wash their knives and other tools too. They should keep cold foods cold and hot foods hot. People should eat cooked foods quickly or put them in the refrigerator.

From Food to Energy

Your body digests food when you eat it. Your digestive system breaks down the food so the body can use it. These are the main parts of the digestive system.

- **Mouth** Your teeth break the food into pieces. Your tongue mixes the food with saliva. Now you can swallow the food.
- **Stomach** Your muscles mix the food with juices. The food becomes a sticky paste.
- **Small Intestine** More juices break down the food. The food parts pass through your intestine walls. They go into your blood.
- **Large Intestine** Water gets into your blood. Some food parts are not digested. They form solid waste and leave the body.

© Pearson Education, Inc. 3

Lesson 5 Checkpoint

1. Name three things people need to survive.

_____

_____

2. How can you be sure of getting all the nutrients you need?

_____

_____

_____

3. Write the steps that show how an apple changes from the time you eat it until the time you can use its energy.

_____

_____

_____

_____

_____

_____

_____

Lesson 6: How can people stay healthy?

Vocabulary

germs very small living things or particles

disease a condition in which part of the body does not work properly

Exercise

It is important to remember that exercise helps our bodies stay healthy. Some people do sports for exercise. They bike, swim, or skate. They play basketball or soccer. House work and yard work can be exercise too.

Exercise keeps a person's heart, lungs, and muscles strong. These are parts of the body's systems. Your heart and blood vessels are part of your circulatory system. Your heart pumps blood through the vessels. The vessels carry digested food particles to your body. They also carry away wastes. Your lungs are part of your respiratory system. The respiratory system takes oxygen from the air. It gives the oxygen to your body.

It is important to get a lot of exercise. Exercise gives you the energy to work and play. It makes people feel good about themselves. Then they take care of their bodies. They eat a variety of foods. They get enough exercise and rest. They do not eat foods that are unhealthy.

Avoiding Germs

When you have the flu, you are sick. You sneeze, you cough, and you have a runny nose. Germs cause this illness. **Germs** are very small living things or particles. Bacteria and viruses are germs. They can make people sick. A **disease** is a condition in which part of the body does not work properly. Some common diseases are the flu, chicken pox, and strep throat. Some other diseases are measles, mumps, and whooping cough. Years ago, many people got these diseases. They were dangerous. Today, children get protection from these diseases.

Most illnesses are not dangerous. But no one likes to be sick. So we need to stop the spread of germs. Remember these simple rules to stop spreading germs.

- Stay home when you are sick.
- Wash your hands often. Always wash your hands before and after you touch food.
- Cover your nose and mouth when you sneeze or cough. Then wash your hands.
- Clean cuts and scrapes. Cover them with a bandage.

Lesson 6 Checkpoint

1. Why is exercise important for your body?

_____

_____

2. What does the circulatory system do?

_____

_____

3. Make a list of things you can do to stop the spread of germs.

_____

_____

_____

_____

Lesson 1: Why is water important?

Vocabulary

water vapor water in the form of an invisible gas in the air

groundwater fresh water that is found underground

wetlands areas such as marshes and swamps that are usually soggy
and wet

Living Things and Water

About two-thirds of your body is made of water. Water helps every part of your body. Water helps you live in many ways. Water helps digest food into small particles. Water in your blood carries materials to all parts of your body. Water also carries wastes away.

Water helps keep your body at the right temperature. When the air is cold, water in your body keeps you warm. When your body is very hot, you sweat. The water in sweat takes heat away from your body.

Some organisms spend their whole lives in water. Many of these are very small.

The Uses of Water

All living things need water. Plants use water to make their own food. Fish live in water.

People use water in many ways.

• **Drinking** People need water to drink.
• **Food** People eat fish and plants that live in water.
• **Crops and Farms** Farmers use water to grow crops.
• **Transportation** Ships move goods over water.
• **Industry** Factories use water in many ways. Water is used to clean foods and buildings. Factories use water to make paper and steel. Industry uses more water than farming does. Most of this water is put back into rivers after it is used.
• **Electricity** People use moving water to make electricity. They build dams and power stations across rivers.

We also use water to have fun, like swimming and sailing.

The Planet of Water

Three-fourths of Earth's surface is covered with water. Most of this water is salty ocean water. You cannot drink, wash clothes, or water plants with saltwater.

Water is found in many different places. Some goes into the ground. Other water is frozen as ice. Some is in the air as an invisible gas called **water vapor.** Water vapor rises from oceans and lakes. It mixes with air.

Fresh Water

Fresh water does not have much salt in it. We drink fresh water. Most of the fresh water on Earth is frozen as ice. This ice is near the North and South Poles.

Some of the fresh water that we use comes from under the ground. Water goes into the soil and collects in spaces between underground rocks. This water is called **groundwater.** People dig wells to reach the groundwater. We also get fresh water from lakes, rivers, and streams. This water moves all the time.

Water can move slowly where the ground is low. This makes the ground very wet for at least part of the year. Places with wet or water-covered ground are called **wetlands.** Wetlands are homes for animals. Water in wetlands seeps into the ground to help refill the groundwater supply.

Lesson 1 Checkpoint

1. How does water help you live?

_____

_____

_____

2. List three ways that people use water.

_____

_____

_____

3. **Cause and Effect** What would happen if we did not protect our fresh water supply?

_____

_____

4. Why is fresh water important?

_____

_____

5. What are four sources of fresh water?

_____

_____

Lesson 2: How does water change form?

Vocabulary

evaporation the changing of a liquid into a gas

condensation the changing of a gas into a liquid

water cycle the movement of water from Earth's surface into the air and back again

precipitation water that falls to Earth as rain, hail, sleet, or snow

Forms Water Can Have

Water can be a liquid, a solid, or a gas. Cold weather can freeze water from a liquid to a solid. When water freezes, it takes up more space.

Water can also become a gas. **Evaporation** happens when liquid turns into a gas. The Sun shines on the water. The water evaporates. It becomes water vapor. Water vapor is a gas. It is in the air. You cannot see water vapor, but sometimes you can feel it. Water vapor makes the air feel warm and sticky.

Water vapor can turn back into a liquid. This is called **condensation.** Sometimes we see dew in the morning. Dew is formed by condensation. The air has water vapor in it. At night, the air cools. Condensation turns the water vapor into drops of water. The drops form dew.

How Water Moves Around Earth

Earth has a certain amount of water. We use the water again and again. The **water cycle** is the movement of water from Earth's surface into the air and back again. The water cycle gives us a constant supply of fresh water.

Water moves through the water cycle. It changes form as it moves. The Sun and winds heat the water. It evaporates and becomes water vapor. Water vapor goes up into the cooler air. It cools and turns back into water. This is called condensation. Water droplets join together to form clouds.

When there are a lot of water droplets in the clouds, they get heavy. The droplets fall to Earth. These water droplets are called **precipitation.** Precipitation can be rain, snow, sleet, or hail. The kind of precipitation depends on Earth's temperature. If it is freezing on Earth, the water droplets may freeze and fall as snow. If it is above freezing, the water falls as rain.

Some precipitation goes into the ground. It becomes groundwater. Other precipitation goes into streams, rivers, lakes, and oceans. When the Sun warms the water, it evaporates. The water cycle continues all the time everywhere.

Ways to Clean Water

People must use water that is clean. Water may have salt, dirt, or germs in it. Germs can make people sick. We need to take the germs out of the water before we drink it.

In some places, families clean their own water. They get the water from wells. Then they filter the water. This removes dirt and chemicals.

In cities, people do not clean their own water. The water is cleaned in one place. First, the water moves through pipes. It goes to a water-treatment area. Next, chemicals are added to the water to kill germs. Then the water sits in big tanks. Tiny pieces of dirt fall to the bottom of the tank. This makes the water even cleaner. Finally, the water goes through a filter. Some filters have sand. The sand takes out more dirt. Now, the water is clean. It moves through pipes to our homes.

© Pearson Education, Inc. 3

Lesson 2 Checkpoint

1. What are the three forms of water?

_____

_____

2. Name the main steps in the water cycle.

_____

_____

_____

3. **Cause and Effect** What kind of precipitation would occur if the temperature was above freezing?

_____

_____

4. What properties of water allow the water cycle to take place?

_____

_____

_____

5. Why must water be cleaned?

_____

_____

Name _____

Lesson 1: What makes up weather?

Vocabulary

weather what it is like outside, including temperature, wind, clouds, and precipitation

atmosphere the blanket of air that surrounds Earth

Parts of Weather

Weather is what the air is like outside. Some parts of weather are clouds in the sky and water in the air. The wind and the temperature of the air are also parts of weather.

Clouds are made of water in the air. Weather can change clouds. Clouds look different in different kinds of weather. Clouds are white and fluffy on a warm and sunny day. Clouds are dark on a stormy day.

Measuring Weather

The **atmosphere** is the air that surrounds Earth. It is made of different gases. The atmosphere is like a blanket of air. It wraps around Earth. The atmosphere has different parts, or layers.

The atmosphere holds air and gas. Air and gas have weight. So the atmosphere presses down on Earth. This is called air pressure. High air pressure means the air presses down a lot. Low air pressure means the air presses down a little.

When air pressure changes it tells you about the weather. Low air pressure can mean there will be clouds or rain. High air pressure can mean the sky will be clear.

Scientists use tools to measure the weather. A barometer is a tool to measure air pressure. An anemometer measures the speed of the wind. A wind vane measures the direction of the wind. A hygrometer measures the water vapor in the air. This is called humidity. The humidity is high when the air has a lot of water vapor in it. A rain gauge also measures water. It measures how much rain fell.

Weather Map

Weather tools collect information about the weather. Scientists can show this information on special maps. Weather maps show weather information. They show air temperatures. They show storms. Some weather maps also show air pressure. They show areas of high and low air pressure.

Look at the picture of the weather map on page 178 of your textbook. It shows the United States. The numbers show the temperatures. The small pictures show the type of weather. The picture of the Sun means the weather will be sunny there. The map's key tells you what all the pictures mean.

A lot of weather information comes from satellites. Satellites move high above Earth. Weather satellites get information from all around the world. They send pictures and information to weather scientists. The information tells scientists where the storms are. It tells where the storms are going. The scientists can put this information on weather maps.

Pollution Alerts

People can also have an effect on the weather. Cars and trucks have engines. These engines give off gases called exhaust. Sometimes the exhaust stays in the air. The Sun's rays can turn it into smog and ozone.

A weather report might announce a pollution alert. That means there is a lot of smog and ozone in the air. Air pollution hurts your body. The gases can make people cough. It is hard for some people to breathe. They must stay inside if there is a pollution alert.

Lesson 1 Checkpoint

1. How do clouds look on stormy days?

_____

2. How do tools help scientists describe the weather?

_____

_____

3. ◎ **Make Inferences** High pressure is moving into an area. Use this observation and what you know about air pressure to predict the weather change.

_____

_____

_____

4. What can weather maps show?

_____

_____

5. What is one effect that humans can have on weather?

_____

_____

6. ◎ **Make Inferences** If there is a smog alert, what can you infer about the weather?

_____

_____

_____

Lesson 2: How are weather patterns different?

Vocabulary

hurricane a huge storm that forms over an ocean

tornado a spinning, funnel-shaped column of air that touches the ground

blizzard a winter storm with very low temperatures and blowing snow

Weather Patterns

Changes in weather follow patterns. Weather patterns depend on the Sun, the water, and where you live. A place near the ocean has one weather pattern. A place far from the ocean has a different pattern.

For example, different parts of Washington State have different weather patterns. The western part of Washington State touches the Pacific Ocean. Air over an ocean has lots of water vapor. The wind pushes this air towards and over the land. It moves from west to east. When the water vapor in the air condenses here, it falls as rain. The western valleys of Washington get lots of rain.

As the air keeps moving east, it hits the Cascade Mountains. The air gets pushed up the side of the mountain. Air gets colder as it goes up. When the water vapor condenses here, it falls as snow. The western part of the state has wet and snowy winters.

The eastern part of the state has another weather pattern. Winds have pushed the air over the Cascade Mountains. Much of the water vapor that was in the air is now gone. So the weather is dry.

All deserts are dry, but each desert has its own weather pattern. North America has four desert areas.

The Sonoran Desert is rainy in the summer. It is in the southern part of Arizona and California. It gets some rain in the winter. But most of the rain there falls during the summer. The moist air comes from the Gulf of California. Normally 5 centimeters (2 inches) of rain falls in the summer.

Dangerous Storms

Most storms are not dangerous. They only bring rain. But other storms are dangerous. Severe thunderstorms can be dangerous. They can have lightning. Lightning can strike people or objects. People should find a safe place to stay during a thunderstorm.

A **hurricane** is a huge storm. Hurricanes form over oceans. They have strong winds. They make big waves. They bring a lot of rain. The rain causes a lot of damage. Scientists try to warn us when a hurricane is going to come.

A **tornado** is a spinning column of air. It looks like a funnel. The air touches the ground. Tornadoes form beneath thunderstorm clouds. They are smaller than hurricanes. But the winds are stronger. People need to stay in safe places. They need to stay away from windows.

Heavy rains can cause a flood. Big waves also cause floods. Water from floods can block roads. It can hurt homes. People need to move to higher places to get away from a flood.

A **blizzard** is a winter storm. A blizzard has low temperatures. It has lots of blowing snow. People can get stuck in the snow. They can get too cold to move.

Radio and television can tell us about the weather. Weather reports tell us about dangerous storms. A storm *watch* means that a storm might happen near you. A storm *warning* means that a storm is really close to you. Listen to storm safety reports. Follow directions to stay safe.

© Pearson Education, Inc. 3

Lesson 2 Checkpoint

1. What do weather patterns depend on?

   _____

   _____

2. **Make Inferences** You know that moist air from the Gulf of California causes storms in the Sonoran Desert in summer. What weather does moist air from the Gulf of Mexico cause in the Midwest in summer?

   _____

   _____

3. What part of the State of Washington has a wet and snowy weather pattern in winter?

   _____

   _____

4. What does a severe thunderstorm warning mean?

   _____

   _____

Lesson 1: How do rocks form?

Vocabulary

rocks natural, solid, nonliving materials found in the Earth

mineral natural material that forms from nonliving matter

igneous rock forms from a red-hot mixture of melted minerals and gases

sedimentary rock rock that forms in layers, one layer at a time

metamorphic rock rock that has been changed by heat and pressure

Rocks

Rocks are natural, solid, nonliving materials found in Earth. Rocks are made of one or more **minerals**. You can tell rocks apart by looking at their physical properties. Some physical properties of rocks are color, what minerals they are made of, and texture. Texture is the size of the bits of minerals, or grains, in the rock. Sometimes the grains are so small that you cannot see them. Some rocks have grains that are big enough to see.

Rock Groups

There are three main groups of rocks: igneous rock, sedimentary rock, and metamorphic rock. Rocks in each group are formed in different ways.

Igneous means "from fire." **Igneous rock** forms from a red-hot mixture of melted minerals and gases. If the mixture cools slowly below ground, the mineral grains in the rock may be big enough to see. If the mixture cools quickly above ground or in the ocean, the grains may be too small to see.

Sediment is made up of bits of rocky matter that settle to the bottom of rivers, lakes, and oceans. Over thousands of years, pressure presses the bits into **sedimentary rock**. Sedimentary rock forms one layer at a time. The top layer is the newest. Sedimentary rocks often show the remains of extinct plants and animals. These remains are called fossils.

Metamorphic means "changes form." **Metamorphic rock** is rock that has been changed by heat and pressure. Slate is a metamorphic rock that used to be a sedimentary rock called shale. Rock formed on top of the shale and buried it underground. Heat and pressure changed the minerals in the shale. Then the shale became slate.

© Pearson Education, Inc. 3

Lesson 1 Checkpoint

1. What are some physical properties of rocks?

_____

_____

2. **Compare and Contrast** Look at pages 198 and 199 in your textbook. How are the rocks shown in the pictures alike? How are they different?

_____

_____

_____

3. How is igneous rock that forms above ground different from igneous rock that forms below ground?

_____

_____

_____

4. Describe clues, found in sedimentary rock, which show that living things have changed over time.

_____

_____

_____

_____

Lesson 2: What are minerals?

Identifying Minerals

Rocks are made of minerals. Minerals are the most common solid material found on Earth. We can identify minerals by their properties. The first way is to look at the mineral's color. Some minerals always have the same color. Other minerals can have different colors. For example, the mineral quartz can be pink, purple, yellow, brown, white, or black.

When you rub a mineral on something rough, it may leave a mark or powder. The mark is called a streak. Even if two pieces of the same type of mineral are different colors, the color of their streaks or powders will be the same.

Another way to identify a mineral is by its luster. Luster shows how a mineral reflects light. Minerals can be pearly, silky, greasy, glassy, or dull.

We can also identify a mineral by its hardness. Some minerals are so soft you can scratch them with your fingernail. Talc is a soft mineral. Some minerals are so hard they can only be scratched by a diamond. A diamond is the hardest mineral. Other minerals can be identified by their appearance, or by taste, smell, or touch.

How We Use Minerals

We use minerals every day. The fluoride in our toothpaste comes from the mineral fluorite. The glass in our windows comes from the minerals quartz and feldspar. The salt in our food is the mineral halite. The metal in a fork has minerals. Even the graphite in a pencil is a mineral. Almost everything we use is made from minerals or has minerals in it.

Minerals Keep Us Healthy

The chemicals in minerals keep our bodies healthy. Many of these minerals come from plants. Green, leafy vegetables such as spinach have calcium. Other green vegetables and fruits have iron. The sodium in some vegetables works with the potassium in fruits to help our bodies move and feel right. Vegetables such as green beans contain phosphorous. Almost everything we eat has some minerals in it.

Lesson 2 Checkpoint

1. What are ways to identify minerals?

   _____

   _____

   _____

2. **Compare and Contrast** How are rocks and minerals alike?
   How are they different? Use a graphic organizer to show your
   answer.

   _____

   _____

3. What is a mineral?

   _____

   _____

4. Why are minerals important to your health?

   _____

   _____

   _____

Lesson 3: Why is soil important?

Vocabulary

soil the thin layer of loose material that covers most of Earth's land

decay the natural breaking down of plant or animal remains

nutrient a thing plants need in order to grow

loam soil that is a mixture of sand, silt, and clay

Parts of Soil

Soil is not just dirt. Soil is the material that covers most of Earth's land. Soil develops naturally over a long period of time. Soil has what plants need to be able to grow.

Living things in soil break down the remains of plants and animals. This process is called **decay**. Decay makes the things plants need in order to grow. Each of these things is a **nutrient**. Some minerals also make nutrients. Plants need water and nutrients in order to grow.

Soil Layers

Soil is found in layers. Topsoil is the top layer. It includes bits of rock mixed with the decayed parts of plant and animal remains. These products of decay are called humus. Humus has what plants need to grow.

Subsoil is under topsoil. It is often lighter in color than topsoil because it has less humus. Tree roots grow into the subsoil. Rainwater and pieces of broken rocks may be in the subsoil.

Solid rock is under the two layers of soil. When solid rock breaks apart, it makes material for new soil.

Comparing Soils

Soil in one place is different from soil in another place. One ingredient of soil is rock particles. Different kinds of rock particles make different types of soil. Sand, silt, and clay are the three main types of rock particles found in soil. They are of different sizes. Sand particles are the largest. Clay particles are the smallest.

All soil has the same four ingredients: rock particles, humus, air, and water. Most of the soil is made up of rock particles with minerals. Humus is made of decaying plants and animals. Air and water fill the spaces between the rocks and the humus.

Most soils are a mixture of sand, silt, and clay. Soils with this mixture are called **loam**. Loam soils also have humus. Loam soils are good for growing most plants because loam soils hold on to water. This makes it easier for plant roots to soak up the water and nutrients.

Lesson 3 Checkpoint

1. What is soil made of?

_____

_____

2. Explain the importance of soil.

_____

_____

3. Compare the ability of sand, silt, and clay to hold water.

_____

_____

_____

Lesson 1: What are Earth's layers?

Vocabulary

crust the outer layer of Earth

mantle the layer of Earth beneath the crust

core the innermost layer of Earth

landforms the solid features formed on Earth's crust

Earth's Layers

Earth has three main layers. The layers are the crust, the mantle, and the core.

The **crust** is the outer layer of Earth. You live on the crust. The crust under the continents is about 37 kilometers (23 miles) thick.

The **mantle** is the layer of Earth beneath the crust. The mantle is made of very hot rocks. These rocks are so hot they can flow like oozing toothpaste.

The **core** is the Earth's center. The core is made of metal. The core is very hot. It is hot enough to melt. But the core is packed very tightly. That is why most of it stays solid. Only the outside of the core is liquid.

Shapes on Earth's Surface

Landforms are solid features formed on Earth's crust. Mountains, hills, and valleys are landforms. Earth also has bodies of water.

Many forces shape landforms. Forces can come from above and below Earth's crust. Moving water is the main force. For example, rivers carry pebbles and sand. First, the pebbles and sand cut through the crust under the river. Next, the rivers can flood. After a flood, rivers leave the pebbles and sand on their banks. This is how rivers help make valleys. A valley is a low area. The landforms on each side are higher. Sometimes a river makes a valley. Sometimes a glacier makes a valley.

There are many different landforms and bodies of water on Earth. A glacier is a large landform. It is a body of ice. Glaciers move very slowly. Glaciers form in cold places. Snow and ice pile up. It takes many years to form a glacier.

A plateau is a high plain. A plateau is higher than the land around it.

An ocean is a large body of water. The oceans are made of saltwater. Oceans cover most of Earth's surface.

A lake is a body of water. The water has slowed and filled an area.

A volcano is an opening in Earth's crust. Hot and melted rock comes out of the opening. Pressure inside Earth forces the rock out.

A mountain is a very high landform. It is higher than the land around it. Some mountains form near the cracks in Earth's crust. Blocks of rock near the cracks push up or drop down.

A river is a natural stream of water.

A hill is a high landform. Hills are not as high as mountains. Many hills have round tops.

A plain is a large area. It is mostly flat.

A coast is where the land meets the ocean.

Lesson 1 Checkpoint

1. What is Earth's core like?

_____

_____

2. Contrast Earth's crust, mantle, and core.

_____

_____

_____

3. **Sequence** List the events that occur as rivers move through rock.

_____

_____

_____

Lesson 2: What are volcanoes and earthquakes?

Vocabulary

magma hot, melted rock under pressure from gases within it

lava hot, molten rock that erupts from a volcano

How Do Volcanoes Form?

The mantle is the layer of Earth under the crust. Volcanoes begin deep in Earth's mantle. **Magma** forms deep in the mantle. Magma is hot, melted rock. There are also gases in magma. The gases put magma under pressure. This pressure can push magma up into the crust. A volcano is an opening on Earth's surface. If there is a weak spot in the crust, the magma will come out. An eruption is hot material pushing from the mantle up to Earth's surface.

The gas forces the magma up in an eruption. Hot material comes out. This material has ash, cinders, and **lava**. Lava is hot, molten rock. The rock is so hot it is a liquid. Lava turns back to solid rock when it cools. The rock can build to form a mountain or island.

Volcanoes

A magma chamber is a large area of magma. Magma chambers are in Earth's mantle. Magma pushes up a tunnel through cracks and weak spots in Earth's crust when it leaves the chamber. This tunnel is also called a vent. Most magma goes out of a vent at the top of the volcano. This vent is called the crater.

Before a volcano erupts, it has magma deep underground in the magma chamber in Earth's mantle. Next the pressure pushes the magma up. The magma is pushed out of weak spots in Earth's crust. Now the magma is called lava. The lava becomes rock when it cools. The rock builds up. If it is high enough, it can form a mountain.

Earthquakes

Earth's crust has parts that usually move slowly. Sometimes they can move a lot. A big move will make the ground shake. This is called an earthquake. Most earthquakes happen near a fault. A fault is a large crack in Earth's crust.

Earthquake Damage

Earthquakes cause damage if they are close to Earth's surface. They cause more damage if they last a long time. Earthquakes near cities can damage buildings, bridges, and underground pipes.

Earthquakes can also cause landslides. The land slides down a slope and rocks and earth fall down. Landslides can happen on land or on the ocean floor. Landslides on land can damage homes and roads. They can bury large areas. Landslides under water can cause huge waves.

Lesson 2 Checkpoint

1. What does lava become when it cools?

   _____

   _____

2. Compare and contrast magma and lava.

   _____

   _____

3. Where do most earthquakes happen? Why?

   _____

   _____

4. **Sequence** Use a graphic organizer to show the steps in the eruption of a volcano.

Lesson 3: What are weathering and erosion?

Vocabulary

weathering any action that breaks rocks into smaller pieces

erosion the movement of weathered material

Weathering

Landforms change when rocks break apart. **Weathering** is any action that breaks down rocks. Weathering breaks rocks into smaller pieces. Weathering takes a lot of time. Some changes take less than a year. Some changes take hundreds of years.

Plants can cause weathering. Plant roots grow into the ground. The roots grow and break up the soil and rock. Sometimes water mixes with decayed materials in the soil. Then the water can change. This water weathers rock in a special way. The water changes the minerals in the rock under the soil. When the minerals change, they weaken the rocks and it breaks apart.

Water also causes weathering. When water gets into a crack in a rock, the water freezes. Frozen water takes up more space. The ice pushes against the crack. After some years, the rock splits apart.

Ice also causes another kind of weathering. Ice makes glaciers. Glaciers are huge areas of ice and snow that move slowly on Earth's crust. Rocks and ice scrape against the land when glaciers move. Some land is scraped away. Glaciers scrape open valleys. There are many rocks of all sizes on the ground after a glacier melts.

Erosion

Weathering can also move materials. **Erosion** is the movement of weathered materials. Water, wind, gravity, and glaciers cause erosion. Weathering and erosion change landforms.

Water causes the erosion that weathers most landforms. Rivers carry bits of rock to new places. Sometimes, rivers carry rock and soil from the land to the ocean. These particles can build up over time. This kind of erosion can form new islands. Rainwater also causes erosion. It takes soil away from hills and high places. Waves cause erosion near shorelines.

Wind causes erosion in dry places such as deserts. The wind picks up dry sand and soil. It blows them to new places. The particles scrape against the desert rocks. They break off tiny pieces, and over time the desert rocks break down and change.

Living things can cause erosion. Animals that live or work in the ground mix and move soil. They move it from one layer to another. This helps water and air move into the ground.

Gravity can cause erosion because it pulls rocks and soil downhill. Mudflows and rockslides are kinds of erosion that happen quickly. Gravity pulls wet soil down in a mudslide. It pulls rocks down in a rockslide.

Lesson 3 Checkpoint

1. Describe weathering, giving three examples.

   _____

   _____

2. How are weathering and erosion different? How are they alike?

   _____

   _____

3. How does most erosion happen in dry regions?

   _____

   _____

Lesson 1: What are resources?

Vocabulary

natural resources important materials from the Earth that living things need

renewable resources resources that can be replaced in a fairly short time

nonrenewable resources resources that cannot be replaced

Resources That Can Be Replaced

The things we need come from **natural resources.** Some natural resources can be replaced. For example, trees and crops grow on Earth's surface. Trees and crops need air and water. Water comes from rain, rivers, lakes, and groundwater. Air is everywhere above ground.

People cut down trees for wood. They use the wood to build houses and make paper. People can plant new trees to replace the trees they cut down. Natural resources that can be replaced are called **renewable resources.** Trees are a renewable resource.

Resources That Cannot Be Replaced

Many natural resources come from below the ground. Miners dig into the ground to get rocks called ores. Ores are important natural resources because they contain metals or other minerals that people use. Copper and iron are useful metals.

People use iron to make steel. A bus is made of steel. A fork is made of steel too. Iron is very useful. But we cannot replace iron ore after we use it. **Nonrenewable resources** are natural resources that cannot be replaced.

Coal is another nonrenewable resource. Coal is a fuel, like oil and natural gas. Fuels give off useful energy when they are burned. Energy from fuel heats buildings. Fuel makes cars and trucks work. Energy from fuel can only be used once. We need to dig deep in the ground to get more fuel. But there is only a certain amount of fuel in the ground. We cannot replace fuel once we use it.

Sometimes, we use up all the ore, minerals, or fuel that are in one place. Then we must find new places that hold these resources. Digging into the ground can leave marks in the Earth. This can change the surface of Earth forever.

An Endless Supply of Resources

Some natural resources are not used up. For example, plants get a lot of sunlight. The Earth can clean the air we breathe. The Earth can also clean the water we drink. Sunlight, air, and water are resources that are always found on Earth.

© Pearson Education, Inc. **3**

Lesson 1 Checkpoint

1. What makes some resources renewable?

_____

2. List two nonrenewable resources.

_____

_____

3. Why is coal a nonrenewable resource?

_____

_____

4. **Compare and Contrast** How are renewable and nonrenewable resources alike? How are they different?

_____

_____

_____

_____

Lesson 2: How can we protect our resources?

Vocabulary

conservation the wise use of natural resources

Using Resources Responsibly

You can save fuel by riding on a bus instead of in a car. You can choose products that come wrapped in less paper and plastic. This makes less garbage. Saving in these ways is called conservation. **Conservation** is the smart use of natural resources so that people do not waste, damage, or use them up.

Clean water is an important resource. We can conserve water by using less. For example, you can turn off the water while you brush your teeth.

Communities conserve water by cleaning it. For instance, wetlands clean dirty water. Water is piped into wetlands. Soil in the wetlands takes harmful particles out of the water. Then plants and other living things break down these particles. Finally, the water is clean. It can flow back into a river and be used again.

Soil is another resource that we must use carefully. Water and wind wash away soil. This is called erosion. Soil needs to be protected from erosion. Some farmers try to protect the soil. These farmers plant crops around hills. The curved rows of plants hold back rainwater. The soil soaks up the water instead of being washed away. Farmers also plant trees next to fields. This keeps soil from blowing away.

Using Up Land Space for Trash

Everything we use is made from natural resources. For example, plastic milk jugs are made from oil. Food cans are made from metals, like steel and tin. We throw these things away after we use them. They become trash. Trash never really goes away. Most garbage goes to a landfill. Trash lays on top of a liner to keep pollution from leaking into the groundwater. More trash is brought to the landfill every day.

Landfills are filling up. But people still need to bury trash. How can we reduce landfill space? One way is by burning garbage. Garbage can be burned in special furnaces. Burning garbage creates energy that can be used to heat buildings and make electricity. But smoke from burning garbage can harm the air. The smoke must be cleaned. Special smoke cleaners are expensive.

We can also reduce landfill space by making less garbage. What are some ways we can reduce the amount of garbage?

© Pearson Education, Inc. 3

Quick Study

Lesson 2 Checkpoint

1. Describe ways people can conserve water.

_____

_____

_____

_____

2. Where does most garbage go after it is taken from your home?

_____

3. What are some ways to save landfill space?

_____

_____

Lesson 3: What are ways to use resources again?

Vocabulary

recycle change something so that it can be used again

Using Resources Again

We conserve resources when we reuse things. For example, you can reuse cloth napkins. You cannot reuse paper napkins. You can reuse empty jars. You can give toys and clothes that you no longer use to other people.

Another way to conserve resources is to **recycle.** You recycle when you change something so that it can be used again. Metal, glass, plastic, and paper are four main kinds of materials that are recycled. Reusing and recycling these materials keeps more land from being used as landfills. This conserves land.

In Lesson 2, you learned how water is conserved and recycled. Like water, glass may also be cleaned and reused. Unlike water, glass is brought to a recycling plant. Workers sort the glass by color. Most jars are clear, brown, or green. Bottles and jars are broken into pieces called shards. The shards are sent to glass companies. The shards must pass under a magnet. The magnet takes off any metal that might be on the glass. Then the shards are crushed into tiny pieces called cullet. The cullet is cleaned and dried. Now the cullet can be turned into new glass things. The cullet is melted in furnaces. Machines blow the cullet into glass bottles and jars. Some glass is used to make windows. Glass can be recycled many times.

Using Recycled Materials

Many communities collect items to be recycled. These items are picked up with the regular garbage. Some places have special containers for bottles and cans. Grocery stores collect used plastic shopping bags to recycle.

You can shop for things made from recycled materials. You might buy a new winter jacket. Some jackets have stuffing in them. Some of this stuffing is made from shredded milk jugs. Or you might play on a playground that has a surface made out of shredded car tires.

The Three *R's*

What is a good way to remember what you have learned about protecting natural resources? Remember the three *R's*—reduce, reuse, and recycle. *Reduce* the amount of resources you use and the trash you make. *Reuse* old things in new ways. *Recycle* everything you can. Doing these things helps you care for the Earth.

© Pearson Education, Inc. 3

Lesson 3 Checkpoint

1. What are the four main types of materials that are recycled?

_____

_____

2. ⊙ **Compare and Contrast** How is recycling glass the same as recycling water? How does recycling glass differ from recycling water?

_____

_____

_____

3. Why is it important to recycle?

_____

_____

4. What are the three *R's*?

_____

_____

_____

Lesson 1: How can we describe matter?

Vocabulary

matter anything that takes up space and has weight

property something about matter you can observe with one or more of your senses

pressure pushing caused by air

element matter made of a single type of particle that is too small to see

atom the smallest particle of an element with properties of that element

periodic table an arrangement of elements based on their properties

Everything you see is made of matter. **Matter** is anything that takes up space and has weight. You can feel the weight of something when you pick it up. Even air takes up space.

A **property** is something about matter that you can see, feel, hear, touch, or smell. You see that a ball is round. You hear it bounce on the floor. You can smell a flower. These things are properties.

There are three states of matter: solid, liquid, or gas. Each kind of matter is made of very small pieces called particles that you cannot see. Particles are always moving.

Ice is a solid. A solid is a kind of matter. Solid particles are packed close together and move very fast. But they stay in place.

Ice can change from a solid to a liquid. Ice can melt into water. Water is a liquid. Liquid particles are loosely connected and can move past each other. Water takes the shape of the glass it is poured into. Pretend you pour water from the glass into another container. The water will change shape again. The water will take up the same amount of space in the new container.

Water can change from a liquid to a gas when it evaporates. Air is a gas. You can pump air into a basketball. The air will fill the space inside the basketball. Air has no shape. Gas particles are tiny. They are not connected to each other. The particles move around freely. The amount of space that air takes up changes. It spreads out to fill space.

Air expands when it is pumped into a basketball. It will push against the inside of the ball until the ball is filled. This pushing is called pressure. You can feel the **pressure** by pushing on the ball before and after air is added.

An **element** is matter that is made of one kind of particle. Gold is an element. A piece of gold is only made of gold particles.

But most objects are not elements because they are made of many types of particles that can be joined in many ways. The smallest particle of an element that has the properties of that element is an **atom.** Gold is made of gold atoms. Clay is made of different types of atoms.

There are more than 100 different elements. Scientists sort these elements in a **periodic table.** Elements are arranged based on their properties. Elements with similar properties are near each other in the periodic table.

© Pearson Education, Inc. 3

Lesson 1 Checkpoint

1. What is *matter*?

_____

_____

2. What are three states of matter?

_____

_____

3. ◎ **Cause and Effect** How does melting ice into water, and then letting the water evaporate, change the state of the ice?

_____

_____

_____

4. Explain why most objects you observe are not elements.

_____

_____

5. What about elements is used to arrange them in the periodic table of the elements?

_____

_____

Lesson 2: How are properties of matter measured?

Vocabulary

mass the amount of matter an object has

volume the amount of space that an object takes up

density a measure of the amount of matter in a certain amount of space

buoyancy the ability of matter to float in a liquid or gas

Mass is the amount of matter an object has. We use a balance to measure mass. We measure mass in units called grams (g). Larger amounts of matter are measured in kilograms (kg). There are 1,000 grams in a kilogram.

If you cut one piece of wood into two pieces, the two pieces together still have the same mass as the whole piece. But, an object's weight is different in different places.

Volume is the amount of space an object takes up. We use a measuring cup or graduated cylinder to measure volume. These tools have numbers on their sides. The numbers show how much liquid there is. A liquid's volume is measured in liters (L) and milliliters (mL). There are 1,000 milliliters in a liter.

A solid's volume can be measured using water. To measure the volume of a small rock, you need to fill a measuring cup half way with water. Write down how many milliliters of water there are in the cup. Then put the rock in the water. Write down the new water level. Subtract the first number from the second number. This is the volume of the rock.

Density is the amount of matter in a certain amount of space. You can study an object's density by seeing how well the object floats in a liquid or gas. This is called **buoyancy**. Stones sink in water. They have little buoyancy. This means stones have a higher density than water. Helium is a gas. Balloons filled with helium rise in the air. Helium has a lot of buoyancy. This means that helium has a lower density than air.

You can also compare the density of two solid objects with the same volume. Find a bowling ball and a rubber ball of the same size. The bowling ball is harder to lift. The bowling ball has more mass. This means the bowling ball also has greater density.

Size is another property that can be measured. Length is the distance from one end of an object to the other end. We can measure length using metric rulers and tapes. Length can be measured in meters (m), centimeters (cm), or millimeters (mm). There are 100 cm in a meter. There are 1,000 mm in a meter. We measure long distances in kilometers (km). There are 1,000 meters in a kilometer.

Other tools and units can be used to measure the volume of solid objects. A cubic unit is a cube used to measure volume. For example, you want to find the volume of a box. You need to find out how many cubes of one size would fit inside the box. A cube that is 1 centimeter on each side has a volume of 1 cubic centimeter. If 12 cubes fill the box, the volume is 12 cubic centimeters.

© Pearson Education, Inc. 3

Quick Study

Lesson 2 Checkpoint

1. How are an object's mass and weight different?

_____

_____

2. **Cause and Effect** What effect would cutting a piece of wood in half have on the total mass of the wood?

_____

_____

3. What is *density*?

_____

_____

4. Describe how you would measure the volume of a liquid.

_____

_____

_____

5. How could you measure the volume of a box?

_____

_____

Lesson 1: What are physical changes in matter?

Vocabulary

physical change a change that makes matter look different without becoming a new substance

states of matter the forms of matter—solid, liquid, and gas

Making a Physical Change

Matter goes through a **physical change** when it changes the way it looks without becoming a new kind of matter. For example, the bits of rock look different than a mountain. But each bit is still made of the same matter as the mountain.

Cutting fruit into pieces causes a physical change. The pieces of fruit are made of the same matter as the whole fruit. You also make a physical change when you fold clothes. Cutting paper, folding paper, and tearing paper are all physical changes too.

Some Ways to Cause Physical Change

There are many ways to change how matter looks. One kind of physical change is a change in the state of matter. **States of matter** are the forms that matter can take: solid, liquid, and gas. Matter can change state between solid, liquid, or gas. The matter stays the same even if the state of the matter changes. For example, liquid water freezes to become ice. Ice is a solid. You can see the ice is still water when it melts. Ice and water are the same kind of matter.

A change in temperature can change the state of matter. For example, water evaporates quickly when it is heated to 100°C (212°F). This means the water changes from a liquid into a gas. The water particles stay the same. But now the particles are so far apart that you cannot see them in the air. This is a physical change.

Water also changes state when it is cooled. The particles of liquid water slide past each other when the water is above 0°C (32°F). Water changes from a liquid to solid ice at or below 0°C. Each water particle slows down and quickly moves back and forth in one place.

What happens when you hold an ice cube in your hand? The heat from your hand makes the water particles move faster. The particles flow as liquid water. You can make physical changes to matter, but the amount and kind of matter stay the same.

Lesson 1 Checkpoint

1. Describe a physical change in matter and explain why it is a physical change.

   _____

   _____

2. List ways that you can make physical changes in matter.

   _____

   _____

   _____

3. What physical changes happen to water as it freezes?

   _____

   _____

   _____

4. 🎯 **Cause and Effect** Make a graphic organizer like the one on page 301 of your textbook. Fill it with ways to cause physical changes to a piece of paper. Describe the effects each change would have on the paper.

Lesson 2: What are some ways to combine matter?

Vocabulary

mixture two or more kinds of matter that are placed together

solution a mixture in which one or more substances dissolves in another

Mixtures

A bowl filled with different kinds of beans is a mixture. A **mixture** is made of two or more kinds of matter that are placed together. Each kind of matter in a mixture does not change into another substance. Each kind of matter can be separated from the other matter in the mixture.

Some mixtures are very easy to separate. For example, you can separate sand grains and marbles because of their size. You can put the mixture in a strainer with small holes. The marbles are too big to go through the holes. But the sand goes right through.

Solutions

Have you ever mixed lemonade powder into water to make lemonade? You stir the powder into the water. The powder seems to disappear. But it doesn't go away. It dissolves. This means the powder breaks into particles so tiny that you cannot see them. The particles spread evenly through the water.

A **solution** forms when you dissolve one or more substances into another. A solution is a kind of mixture. You might not see the particles in a solution. You might not be able to see the powder in the lemonade. But you know it's there when you taste it.

You can separate the parts of a solution. Think about ocean water. Ocean water is salty. How can you separate the salt from the water? You cannot use a strainer. The salt particles are too small to be trapped by the strainer.

What if you heat the saltwater until it boils? The water evaporates. The salt separates from the water. The salt is left behind in the pot. The same thing happens with lemonade. The powder stays behind after the water evaporates.

These separations are physical changes. The changes may make the substance look different. But the substances are still the same.

Lesson 2 Checkpoint

1. Give three reasons why a bowl of different kinds of beans is a
mixture.

_____

_____

_____

2. What makes ocean water a mixture?

_____

_____

3. What makes ocean water a solution?

_____

_____

Lesson 3: What are chemical changes in matter?

Vocabulary

chemical change a change that causes one kind of matter to become a different kind of matter

Forming Different Materials

In a **chemical change**, one kind of matter changes into a different kind of matter. A chemical change happens when bread is baked. The batter is a mixture of flour, baking powder, and eggs. But the heat of the oven makes the chemical change happen. Then bread forms.

Remember that water can freeze into ice. Ice can melt back to water. This is a physical change. The water and ice are the same material. What about the flour, baking powder, and eggs that make up the bread? Can you separate these materials from the bread? No. Materials that have gone through a chemical change cannot be changed back to the original kind of matter.

Some chemical changes can happen quickly. For example, fire can burn wood in minutes. The wood changes to gases and ashes. These gases and ashes cannot change back into wood.

Some chemical changes happen slowly. Think about an iron chain that is left outside. Water helps the iron combine with oxygen from the air. This causes the iron to change into rust. The rust is a different kind of matter. The rust cannot change back into iron.

Using Chemical Changes

We use many chemical changes every day. Chemical changes happen in your mouth as soon as you chew a piece of food. More changes happen as the food moves through your body. These chemical changes give your body what it needs to grow.

Chemical changes also help us move from place to place. Burning gasoline is a chemical change. This change releases energy that a car's engine uses.

Chemical changes make many things in life easier to do. For example, laundry soap causes chemical changes that break down stains. Clothes would get dirtier and dirtier without these changes.

Chemical changes also provide us with electricity. For example, chemicals combine inside batteries. This chemical change makes electricity. This electricity helps you use your CD player.

Lesson 3 Checkpoint

1. How do you know that burning wood is a chemical change?

_____

_____

2. **Cause and Effect** Let's say you paint an iron door the color of iron rust. Meanwhile, the bread you are baking turns a rust color on top. Which is a physical change? Which is a chemical change? Explain.

_____

_____

_____

_____

3. What are four ways chemical changes are useful?

_____

_____

_____

_____

4. Does using a battery cause a physical change or a chemical change? Explain your answer.

_____

_____

Lesson 1: What happens when things change position?

Vocabulary

position the location of an object

motion when an object keeps changing position

relative position the position of one object compared with the position of other objects

speed the rate, or how fast, an object changes its position

When Things Move

You can tell that something is moving if it changes its location. It is not standing still. For example, think of a top spinning. You can tell it is moving because it is changing its location. It has changed its **position.** The top is in **motion** because it keeps changing its position.

Ways of Looking at an Object's Position

Sometimes it is hard trying to get somewhere. A map can help you find where you are going. A map is a drawing of a place. A map shows the position of things and places. For example, a map of your school might show the cafeteria and the library. To tell a friend how to get to the cafeteria, you can use words such as *forward, left, right,* and *behind.*

Positions of Moving Objects

The position of each place on a map is relative to other places. *Relative* can mean one thing depends on another thing for its meaning. When you explain how to go to the cafeteria, what you say depends on your position. For example, you might say, "Turn left after the library." **Relative position** is the position of an object compared to the position of other objects.

Look at the picture on page 329 of your textbook. The relative position of car 64 is in front of the other cars. Its position depends on the position of the other cars.

Look at the picture of the train moving on the tracks. The locomotive is in front of the two cars. It is pulling the cars. But if the train stopped and then went backwards, the cars would be moving in front of the locomotive. The direction the train is moving in changes the relative position of the locomotive.

How Fast Things Move

Speed is how fast an object is moving. Speed can be fast or slow. A jet plane moves very fast. A caterpillar moves very slowly.

Constant Speed

When something is moving at a constant speed, its speed does not change. For example, if a car is moving at 35 miles an hour, its speed stays the same.

Variable Speed

Variable speed means that the speed changes. An object that is going at a variable speed changes speed as it moves. For example, look at the picture on page 331. If you were in one of the bumper cars, you could change speed and direction. You could go backward, forward, to the side, or in a circle. The cars move at a variable speed and can go faster or slower.

© Pearson Education, Inc. 3

Lesson 1 Checkpoint

1. How can you tell something is in motion?

_____

_____

2. In what ways can the relative position of an object change?

_____

_____

3. List at least three different ways objects can move.

_____

_____

_____

4. What are four kinds of speed?

_____

_____

_____

_____

5. **Summarize** Write a sentence that summarizes what relative position is.

_____

_____

_____

Use with pp. 332–337

Lesson 2: How does force affect motion?

Vocabulary

force any push or a pull

friction a contact force that opposes the motion of an object

gravity a non-contact force that pulls objects toward each other

magnetism a non-contact force that attracts objects with iron

The Causes of Motion

When you push or pull a door open, you are using force. A **force** is any push or pull. A force can change an object's position. A force can also change the direction an object is moving in.

Most forces are contact forces. This means something touches the object. When you hit a baseball with a bat, the force of the bat changes the direction and the speed of the ball. The bat must touch, or make contact with, the ball. This is a contact force. How much an object changes its position and speed depends on how much force you use. If you push harder on a moving shopping cart, it will go faster.

An object's mass also affects how much it moves. It takes less force to push an empty cart, because it has less mass. When you fill the cart, it has more mass. Then you need to use more force to move it.

When you push the cart down the aisle, its wheels rub against the floor. This creates friction. **Friction** is a contact force that opposes an object when it moves. Friction can make moving objects slow down or stop.

The amount of friction between two objects depends on the kind of surface. It is easy to push a grocery cart over a smooth tile floor. You need more force to push it across an asphalt parking lot. The smooth tile floor creates less friction against the wheels than the asphalt from the parking lot.

Motion and Combined Forces

Have you ever played tug-of-war? Two teams pull on the ends of a rope. Your team pulls in one direction. The other team pulls in the other direction. Both teams are putting a force on the rope. The rope will move in the direction with the stronger combined force.

When you ride a bicycle, many forces make it move. Your legs push the pedals. Friction between the bicycle's tires and the ground slows the bicycle. When you go uphill, you need to use more force. When you go downhill, you may need to use the brakes to slow down. Each force has its own amount and acts in its own direction. All the forces must combine to keep the bicycle moving.

Gravity and Magnetism

A non-contact force is a push or pull that can move an object without touching it.

Gravity is a non-contact force. Gravity pulls objects toward each other without touching then. Gravity pulls everything on Earth toward Earth's center. The pull of gravity on an object depends on how much mass it has. The pull of gravity is greater if the object has more mass.

Magnetism is another non-contact force. Magnets attract metals that have iron in them. For example, a magnet pulls steel paper clips to it. The magnet doesn't need to touch the paper clips.

Quick Study

Lesson 2 Checkpoint

1. What is a force?

_____

_____

2. What two things about forces are important when forces are combined?

_____

_____

3. What are three contact forces?

_____

_____

_____

4. What are two non-contact forces?

_____

_____

Lesson 3: How do simple machines affect work?

Vocabulary

work to use a force and move an object

Work

In science, *work* has a special meaning. You do **work** when you use a force and move an object. You do work when you move a shopping cart, rake leaves, or carry out the trash. You do work when you ride your bike or kick a ball. The amount of work is how much force you use and how far you move the object.

No work is done if an object's position does not change. If you push a big snowball but it does not move, no work is done.

How much work do you do in one day? To answer this, add up how much pushing and pulling you do. Then measure how far you moved things. If you push your desk, that is a certain amount of work. If you push your desk twice as far, that is twice as much work.

Some Simple Machines

Machines don't lessen work, but they help make work easier.

An inclined plane is a surface that slants. A ramp is an inclined plane. It connects a lower level to a higher level. It is easier to push a heavy object up a ramp than to pick it up. It takes less force over a longer distance. This is the same amount of work, but it takes less force to move the object.

A wedge splits, cuts, or connects things. A wedge is made of one or two slanted sides that come together in a sharp edge. Some examples of wedges are a knife that cuts a pie or a nail that goes through a piece of wood.

A screw is an inclined plane that is wrapped around a center post. Look at the picture on page 341 of your textbook. It shows a spiral slide. The slide is wrapped around the center post. The slide is like a screw. Screws can hold things together. They can raise and lower things. For example, the lid of a jar is a screw. It goes up if you turn it one way. It goes down when you turn it the other way.

A lever is a stiff bar that rests on a support. A seesaw is an example of a lever. A lever is used to lift and move things. If you push down on one side of the bar, you can raise an object on the other side.

More Simple Machines

When you turn a doorknob to open a door, you are using a wheel and axle. The knob is a wheel. The post in its center is an axle. You turn the doorknob, or wheel. This is easier than turning the axle. A Ferris wheel and a merry-go-round use a wheel and axle. The motor in these rides turns the axle. The axle then turns the wheel.

A pulley is a simple machine. It changes the direction of how something moves. For example, sailors on a sailboat use a pulley to raise the sail. The top of the sail is attached to a pulley. The pulley has a grooved wheel that is attached to an axle. A rope goes around the pulley. The sailors pull on the rope to turn the grooved wheel. When they pull down on the rope, the sail is pulled up to the top of the pole.

© Pearson Education, Inc. 3

Lesson 3 Checkpoint

1. What is work?

_____

_____

2. What is an inclined plane?

_____

_____

3. **Summarize** State briefly how using an inclined plane makes work easier.

_____

_____

4. How do you know when a simple machine has done work?

_____

_____

5. What simple machine has a grooved wheel, an axle, and a rope?

_____

_____

6. **Summarize** Write a sentence that summarizes how simple machines are useful.

_____

_____

Lesson 1: What is energy?

Vocabulary

potential energy stored energy that has the ability to change in order to do work or cause a change

kinetic energy the energy of motion

Energy

Energy is the ability to do work or cause change. Work is done when a force makes an object move. You have learned about the Sun's energy. Earth gets heat energy and light energy from the Sun. The Sun's heat energy warms the Earth. The Sun's light energy makes plants grow. The Sun's energy also causes winds to blow. It causes water to move through a cycle too.

You use energy from the Sun every day. You also use many other forms of energy. Electrical energy runs many things in your kitchen. Chemical energy runs the engine of a car. The mechanical energy of the car's motion moves you from one place to another.

Stored Energy

Think about a person on skis. The skier uses energy to ski. The skier's body stores this energy. Stored energy is a kind of **potential energy.** Potential energy can change into a different kind of energy in order to do work or cause change.

Fuels are sources of energy. Oil, coal, natural gas, and gasoline are fuels. The energy stored in these fuels comes from sunlight. Long ago, plants used energy from the Sun to make food. Then the plants died. They turned to a kind of fossil that we now use as fuel. We release the potential energy in the fuels when we burn them.

You also release potential energy when you use batteries. The stored energy in fuels, batteries, and food is chemical energy.

A skier at the top of a hill has another kind of potential energy. This kind of potential energy comes from height or position. Picture a swing at its highest point. This swing also has potential energy.

Energy of Motion

Potential energy can also turn into kinetic energy. **Kinetic energy** is the energy of motion. For example, stored energy in gasoline can change into kinetic energy. This energy allows a car to move. A skier standing at the top of a hill pushes off in order to move. This is when the skier's stored potential energy changes to kinetic energy. The force of gravity then pulls the skier down the hill.

Many kinds of energy can be renewed. The skier can get more energy by eating food. The skier can also climb the hill again. Other kinds of energy cannot easily be renewed. For example, gasoline, natural gas, coal, and other fossil fuels are not renewable.

Lesson 1 Checkpoint

1. What are two forms of energy that Earth gets from the Sun?

_____

_____

2. What are two kinds of potential energy?

_____

_____

3. Give two examples of potential energy and kinetic energy that you see every day.

_____

_____

_____

_____

4. **Main Idea and Details** Use a graphic organizer. What is the main idea of the first paragraph under "Energy of Motion"? What details support it?

Use with pp. 362–365

Lesson 2: How does energy change form?

Changing Forms of Energy

Energy can change from one form into another. For example, living things store potential energy as chemical energy. Chemical energy in your body changes to mechanical energy and heat energy as you move. Potential energy can also change into the forms listed below:

- **Chemical energy** This energy holds particles of matter together. Food and fuel contain chemical energy.
- **Mechanical energy** This is the energy of moving objects. Moving parts in machines use kinetic energy. Your body also uses mechanical energy when it moves.
- **Electrical energy** This energy can pass through wires made of special metal. We use this energy to power many machines.
- **Light energy** We see the Sun's energy as light. Plants use light energy to make food.
- **Thermal energy** This form of energy makes particles move faster. We feel thermal energy as heat.

Using Energy

When you turn on a light, this helps change electrical energy to light energy. The light bulb will get hot. This is because some of the electrical energy changes to heat energy. Energy cannot change completely from one form to another. Some energy is given off as heat.

People also use machines to change forms of energy. An electric toothbrush can change chemical energy into electrical energy. It changes electrical energy to mechanical energy when the toothbrush is turned on.

Ways That Energy Travels

Energy can travel from one place to another. A moving object carries energy. For example, you can feel the energy a moving ball is carrying when you catch it.

Energy can also travel as waves. Look at the rope on page 365 in your textbook. A person is moving the rope from side to side. This makes energy move along the rope in waves. Light energy and kinetic energy move in waves.

Energy in water moves in waves. These waves can be small. Waves caused by hurricanes can be huge. The size of a wave depends on how much energy it carries. Waves lose strength as they move away from their source.

Parts of a Wave

You can measure the amount of energy that a wave carries. One way you can do this is by measuring the width of a wave. The width is the distance between the bottom of the wave to the top of the wave. The bottom of a wave is called a trough. The top of a wave is called a crest. Wide waves have lots of energy. Thin waves have less energy.

You can also measure the length of an energy wave. The length of a wave is the distance from the top of one crest to the top of the next crest. Shorter waves have lots of energy. Longer waves have less energy.

Quick Study

Lesson 2 Checkpoint

1. What form of energy do living things change into mechanical energy and thermal energy?

_____

_____

2. Name two types of energy that travel in waves.

_____

_____

3. What happens to energy as it travels away from the source?

_____

_____

4. **Main Idea and Details** Read the first paragraph under "Parts of a Wave." Use a graphic organizer. What is the main idea? What are the supporting details?

Lesson 3: What is heat energy?

Vocabulary

thermal energy the total energy of all the particles in matter; also called heat energy

Heat Energy

All matter is made of very small particles. These particles are always moving. Particles need energy to move. **Thermal energy** is the energy of moving particles.

The Sun is the main source of heat on Earth. Sunlight feels warm on your skin. The sunlight makes your skin's particles move faster. This makes you feel warmer. We feel thermal energy as heat.

Thermal energy moves as heat. It moves from a warmer object to a cooler object. Put a spoon in very hot water. Heat moves from the hot water through the cooler spoon. Soon, the spoon will feel warm. The water and the spoon will reach the same temperature. This is when the flow of energy stops.

Sources of Heat

Heat is given off when energy changes forms. This heat can come from different sources. Four sources of heat are listed below:

- **Electrical Energy** The burner on an electric stove changes electrical energy into heat.
- **Chemical Energy** Burning wood changes chemical energy into heat.
- **Mechanical Energy** Rubbing your hands together keeps your hands warm. This is an example of using mechanical energy to produce heat.
- **Light Energy** The light from the Sun warms Earth. This is an example of light energy changing into heat.

Effects of Heat on Matter

Heat energy changes matter. Energy causes matter to be in a solid, liquid, or gas state. Think about a cup of liquid water. The water turns to ice if the temperature is at or below 0°C (32°F).

What happens when you add heat to ice? Ice starts to melt. Ice becomes a liquid as the temperature warms.

You can measure the effect of heat on matter. You can watch how much time it takes for matter to change from solid to liquid. This change will happen faster when there is greater heat energy.

Water evaporates when enough heat is added to it. Water changes into a gas called water vapor. You cannot see water vapor. Heat makes liquid water change in another way. Heat makes water boil. Water boils at a temperature of 100°C (212°F). A pot of water on top of a stove will change as it heats. This heat makes the water get bigger. Finally, the liquid water evaporates. It changes into a gas. Hot bubbles of gas move to the top of the water. These bubbles break open. They release a cloud of hot water droplets.

Lesson 3 Checkpoint

1. What are four different kinds of heat sources?

_____

_____

_____

_____

2. What is the main source of heat on Earth?

_____

3. What causes matter to be in a solid, liquid, or gas state?

_____

_____

Lesson 4: What is light energy?

Vocabulary

reflect to have light bounce off an object and go in different directions

refract to bend light

absorb to take in

Sources of Light

The Sun, chemical changes, and electricity are three sources of light energy.

The Sun is the main source of light on Earth. Energy moves from the Sun to Earth. The Sun's energy moves as waves. We can see some of these waves. Light is energy that we can see.

Light can also come from chemical changes. Burning is a chemical change. A candle makes light when it burns. A gas lamp makes light as it burns gas. Some animals make light too. The anglerfish can make light. Chemical changes in the fish's body make light.

Electricity is also a source of light. Electricity heats the wire in a light bulb. The wire gets so hot that it glows and gives off light. Most things that give off light also give off heat.

The Path of Light

Light travels from its source in straight lines in all directions. Light is able to travel until an object stops it. Light will not bend in order to get around an object. This is why objects that block light's path form shadows. Shadows are areas behind the objects that are not getting light.

How Light Changes

Some objects block all the light. Light will not go through a brick. Other objects block only part of the light. A window does not block all the light. A glass of water does not block all the light. You can see through these objects.

All objects **reflect** light. This means light bounces off them. The light goes in a different direction. Some objects reflect light better than others. Their surfaces are very flat and smooth. A mirror reflects light. So does a lake's surface.

Some objects **refract** light. Refraction makes light bend and change direction. This can cause objects to look different. Look at the water drops on page 372 in your textbook. The drops refract light from the flower. The rays bend. Tiny images of the flower form.

Why does light refract? Light refracts because it goes through different materials at different speeds. Look at the picture of a straw in water on page 373. Light in the air slows down when it goes through water. The light refracts. That is why the straw looks bent. Sometimes, refraction causes light to separate into its many colors. This makes a rainbow.

Light is made of different colors. Objects **absorb** some of the light. The objects reflect the rest of the colors. Different objects absorb and reflect different colors. A red object in sunlight reflects red light. It absorbs all the other colors. A green object reflects green light. A white object reflects all the colors of sunlight. A black object absorbs all the colors of sunlight. Dark objects feel hot in the Sun. A lot of absorbed sunlight turns to heat.

© Pearson Education, Inc. 3

Lesson 4 Checkpoint

1. Name three sources of light energy.

_____

_____

_____

2. What is the main source of light on Earth?

_____

3. How does a shadow form?

_____

_____

Lesson 5: What is electrical energy?

Vocabulary

electric charge a tiny amount of energy in the particles of matter

electric current the movement of an electric charge from one place to another

electric circuit the path that a controlled, electric current flows through

Electric Charges

All matter is made of small particles. These particles have electric charges. An **electric charge** is a small amount of energy. Particles have positive and negative charges. Particles balance each other out when they have the same number of positive and negative charges. This matter has no charge. When matter has more negative charges than positive charges, this matter has a negative charge. Other matter has more positive charges than negative charges. This matter has a positive charge.

Matter with a negative charge is attracted to matter with a positive charge. The negative charge moves toward the matter with the positive charge. This happens when you touch someone and get a shock. Negative charges jump between you and the other person. Electric charges also create lightning. Light is given off when negative electric charges move in clouds.

Electric charges can make objects stick together. This happens when negative and positive charges are attracted to each other. Rub a balloon on your hair. The balloon will pick up negative charges from your hair. The balloon will stick to paper with a positive charge.

Objects can push away from each other when their charges are the same. Rub two balloons together. They will both have negative charges. The balloons will push apart.

Electric Currents and Circuits

Electric current is the movement of electrical energy. Lightning is an uncontrolled electric current. Controlled electric current travels in a planned way through wires.

An **electric circuit** controls the path that electricity takes. The path must be unbroken for electricity to flow through it. Look at the simple electrical circuit on page 376 in your textbook. The circuit is unbroken when the switch is on. This lets electric current flow from the negative to the positive part of the battery. On its way, it flows through a bulb. A wire in the bulb gets hot and glows. This electrical energy changes to heat and light energy. The current stops flowing when you turn the switch off.

We use electricity every day. So we try to change sources of energy into electricity. We change energy from running water into electricity and turn the heat of burning coal into electricity.

Electricity changes its form when it gets to your house. Electricity can change into:

- **Light** Electricity in light bulbs changes to light.
- **Heat** Electricity moves through coils in heaters and changes into heat.
- **Sound** Electricity moves around a magnet in a radio. The magnet changes electric energy into sound.
- **Magnetic Force** Electricity moves around a huge magnet and makes it very powerful. This magnet can lift cars.

© Pearson Education, Inc. 3

Lesson 5 Checkpoint

1. What causes lightning?

_____

_____

2. What is the difference between a controlled and an uncontrolled electric current? Give an example of each.

_____

_____

_____

3. What happens when an electric circuit is open?

_____

_____

4. **Main Idea and Details** Describe the path of electricity through a simple electric circuit.

_____

_____

Name _____

Lesson 1: What causes sounds?

Vocabulary

vibration a very quick back-and-forth movement

pitch how high or low a sound is

The Causes of Sound

Sounds are all around us. Some sounds are soft, like falling rain. Other sounds are loud, like car horns. Some sounds are nice to hear, like music. Other sounds might bother you or can even hurt your ears. We hear different sounds every day. But all sounds are alike in at least one way. All sounds are made when matter moves.

Sounds happen because matter moves back and forth very quickly, causing movements called **vibrations.** The speed of these vibrations makes sounds different. **Pitch** is how high or low a sound is. Objects that vibrate slowly make sounds with low pitches. Objects that vibrate quickly make sounds with high pitches.

Hitting or Plucking to Make Sound

A drum makes a soft sound when you hit it lightly. A drum makes a louder sound when you hit it harder. The loudness of the sound depends on how much the drumhead moves. The drumhead moves farther back and forth in order to make a louder sound.

Stringed instruments make sounds when they are plucked. All harp strings vibrate when they are plucked. Their vibrations make sounds. Short, thin, and tight strings vibrate quickly. The sounds they make have higher pitches. Longer, thicker strings vibrate more slowly. Their sounds have lower pitches.

Using Air to Make Sound

The sound of your voice also comes from vibrations. You have vocal cords in your throat. The cords vibrate when air passes between them. Your vocal cords also tighten when you speak. The pitch of your voice depends on how tight your vocal cords are. The pitch of your voice is higher when your vocal cords are tighter.

Wind instruments make sounds when air inside them vibrates. You make sounds on a trumpet by blowing into it and vibrating your lips. This makes an air column inside the trumpet vibrate. You can change the trumpet's pitch by changing the length of this vibrating column. You can change the length of the vibrating column by changing how your lips vibrate. You can also press on the trumpet's valves. This changes the length of the vibrating air column inside the trumpet.

© Pearson Education, Inc. 3

Lesson 1 Checkpoint

1. Describe some ways that sounds are alike and different.

_____

_____

_____

2. How is sound made?

_____

_____

3. **Compare and Contrast** How are the sounds produced by different strings of a harp alike and different?

_____

_____

_____

4. What makes the vocal cords vibrate?

_____

_____

5. What are two ways that sound can be different?

_____

_____

Lesson 2: How does sound travel?

Vocabulary

compression wave a wave that has spaces where particles are
squeezed together and spaces where particles are spread apart; sound waves

What are Sound Waves?

Think about the sound of a ringing bell. The bell's vibrations make sound. Sound travels through matter. Air particles are pushed together and spread apart. These moving particles make a **compression wave.** Sound waves are compression waves. The length of a sound wave is measured from the center of one compression to the center of the next compression.

Like the bell, a jackhammer vibrates to make sound. These sound waves spread out in all directions. The sound would be very loud if you were standing near the jackhammer. But the sound waves lose energy when they move away from the jackhammer. The sound is not as loud.

Sound and Matter

You can hear sound only when it travels through matter. Sound moves through gases, liquids, and solids. The speed of a sound wave depends on what kind of matter it is traveling through.

Air is made of gases. The particles in gases are farther apart than in liquids and solids. It takes longer for one gas particle to hit another and move the energy along.

Particles in liquids are closer together. Water is a liquid. This means that sound travels faster in water than in air. Particles in solids are closer together than in liquids. Sound travels fastest in solids.

The Ear

Our ears receive sound waves. They travel on a path to the brain. The brain receives the signals and recognizes them as sounds.

The outer ear collects sound waves. The sound waves hit the eardrum inside the ear. The eardrum vibrates. This makes little bones vibrate inside the ear. These bones are part of the middle ear. The inner ear has a part shaped like a shell. It is filled with liquid. The movement of the tiny bones make the tiny hairs vibrate in the inner ear. The hairs are connected to nerves that carry signals to the brain.

Humans cannot hear all the sounds other animals can hear. Some bats make high-pitched sounds that people cannot hear. Many animals make sounds by using their vocal cords. Many insects make sounds by rubbing body parts together. Other insects make sounds by rubbing their wings together.

Lesson 2 Checkpoint

1. How does sound travel?

   _____

   _____

2. **Compare and Contrast** How are the sound of a jackhammer and the sound of the little bells alike and how are they different?

   _____

   _____

   _____

3. Why does sound travel quickest through solids?

   _____

   _____

4. What path do sound waves follow through the ear?

   _____

   _____

   _____

5. How do some insects make sounds?

   _____

   _____

Lesson 1: What are some patterns that repeat every day?

Vocabulary

> **star** a giant ball of hot, glowing gases
>
> **axis** the imaginary line around which Earth spins
>
> **rotation** one complete spin on an axis

The Sun

Did you know the Sun is a **star**? A star is a giant ball of hot, glowing gases. It is the main source of light and heat for Earth. Earth does not glow or make its own light. It is also much smaller than the Sun. The half of Earth's surface facing the Sun is lit by sunlight. The half of Earth's surface facing away from the Sun is dark.

Day and Night

Earth is moving all the time. One way that Earth moves is by spinning around, or rotating. Earth spins on its axis. An **axis** is an imaginary line. One end of the line sticks out of Earth at the North Pole. The other end of the line sticks out of Earth at the South Pole.

Earth spins in a complete circle every 24 hours. This is called **rotation.** Half of Earth always faces the Sun. That half of Earth has day. The half of Earth that is not facing the Sun has night. As Earth spins, the part of Earth that is in darkness slowly gets more sunlight. A new day begins. At the same time, the part of Earth that was lit by sunlight slowly becomes darker. Daytime ends. This is a pattern that happens every day.

Shadows

Have you ever sat in the shade of a tree? Did you know that you were sitting in a shadow? Three things are needed to see a shadow: light, an object to block the light, and a surface on which the shadow can form.

A shadow forms when light hits an object. The object stops this light. The shadow is an area behind the object that is not getting direct light. The shadow has about the same shape as the object that blocks the light.

The size and shape of shadows change during the day. Shadows are long in the early morning hours. They stretch in the opposite direction of the Sun. This means shadows stretch toward the west. At noon, the Sun is at its highest point in the sky. Shadows are very short. Shadows become long again as the afternoon passes. Now, the shadows stretch toward the east. This is in the opposite direction of the setting Sun. Once the Sun sets, there is no more sunlight to make shadows.

Lesson 1 Checkpoint

1. What star is the source of light on Earth?

_____

2. 🎯 **Sequence** Describe a pattern on Earth that happens every day.

_____

_____

3. What is Earth's axis?

_____

4. Explain how each place on Earth has a beginning and an end to daytime.

_____

_____

5. What three things are needed to have a shadow?

_____

_____

6. 🎯 **Sequence** Describe the pattern of shadows from sunrise to sunset. Include the length and direction of the shadows.

_____

_____

_____

_____

Lesson 2: What patterns repeat every year?

Vocabulary

revolution one complete trip around the Sun

Earth Moves Around the Sun

You know that Earth rotates on its axis as it revolves around the Sun. The axis is an imaginary tilted line through Earth. A **revolution** is one complete trip around the Sun. One revolution takes one year.

Look at Earth's positions on pages 428–429 in your textbook. Earth's tilted axis always points in the same direction as Earth revolves around the Sun. But different parts of Earth tilt toward or away from the Sun. As a result, temperature changes occur throughout the year:

- In June, the northern half of Earth tilts more toward the Sun. The northern half receives more direct sunlight than the southern half. The northern half of Earth is warmer than the southern half. It is summer in the northern half and winter in the southern half of Earth.

- In September, no part of Earth points toward or away from the Sun. The northern half of Earth is becoming cooler while the southern half is becoming warmer.

- In December, the northern half of Earth tilts away from the Sun. It receives less direct sunlight than the southern half. The northern half of Earth is now colder than the southern half. It is winter in the north and summer in the southern half of the Earth.

- In March, both halves of Earth get about the same amount of sunlight. The northern half is getting warmer while the southern half is getting cooler.

Seasons

Earth's tilt and movement cause the amount of sunlight and the temperature to change throughout the year. Usually, temperatures are warmest during the summer and coolest during the winter.

In December, the northern half of Earth is tilted away from the Sun. It is winter in the northern half of Earth.

In March and September, Earth's axis does not point toward the Sun or away from the Sun. Temperatures are usually warmer than in winter but cooler than in summer. Spring and fall happen during these times of the year.

In June, the northern half of Earth tilts more toward the Sun. It is summer in the northern half of Earth.

The Earth's tilt also affects how we see the Sun. The Sun is in different places in the sky during different seasons. In summer, the Sun is higher in the sky. In winter, the Sun is lower in the sky.

Lesson 2 Checkpoint

1. What does Earth revolve around?

_____

2. 🎯 **Sequence** Describe the pattern of temperature changes during the year in the northern half of Earth. Why does this happen?

_____

_____

_____

_____

3. How does Earth's position and movement cause seasons?

_____

_____

4. What causes summer to be warmer than winter?

_____

_____

_____

Lesson 3: Why does the Moon's shape change?

Vocabulary

phase each way the Moon looks from Earth

lunar eclipse when Earth makes a shadow on the Moon

The Moon and Earth

The Moon rotates on its axis and revolves around Earth. It takes about 29 Earth days to complete one revolution. The Moon revolves around Earth while Earth revolves around the Sun.

The Moon is the brightest thing in the night sky. But it does not make light. The Sun lights the Moon. The Sun's light shines on the moon and bounces off. Did you know that we always see the same side of the Moon? We never see the other side from Earth.

The Moon and the Sun

How the Moon looks in the sky changes a little bit each night. Each way the Moon looks is a **phase** of the Moon. The phases always follow the same pattern. It takes about four weeks to complete the entire pattern.

Lunar Eclipse

Sometimes Earth moves between the Sun and Moon. Earth blocks sunlight from the Moon and makes a shadow on the Moon. This is called a **lunar eclipse.** Earth's shadow slowly moves and covers the Moon.

Phases of the Moon

The drawing on page 435 shows the Moon in different positions. You can see that half of the Moon is always lighted by the Sun. We cannot always see this half of the Moon. The amount of the Moon that we can see from Earth is a phase of the Moon.

The first phase is the New Moon. It happens when the Moon gets between the Sun and Earth. Then, the dark half of the Moon faces Earth. The lighted half faces away from Earth. We cannot see the Moon during this phase.

More of the lighted Moon can be seen as the Moon revolves. We see the next phase of the Moon a night or two after the new Moon. This is called the Crescent Moon phase. We can only see a small piece of the lighted part of the Moon.

The Moon looks like a half circle about a week after the New Moon. This is the First Quarter phase.

Finally, we are able to see all of the lighted part of the Moon. The Moon looks like a circle. This is called the Full Moon phase. It happens a week after the First Quarter. We see less of the Moon each night after the Full Moon phase.

Lesson 3 Checkpoint

1. What are two ways the Moon moves? How do these movements affect the appearance of the Moon?

   _____

   _____

2. How much of the Moon is lighted by sunlight?

   _____

3. What position of Earth causes a lunar eclipse?

   _____

   _____

   _____

4. **Sequence** Describe the pattern of the phases of the Moon starting with a full Moon.

   _____

   _____

   _____

   _____

   _____

Lesson 4: What are Star Patterns?

Vocabulary

> **telescope** a tool that magnifies objects that are far away and makes
> them easier to see
>
> **constellation** a group of stars that make a pattern

Stars and the Telescope

Think about the sky on a clear, dark night. You can see lots of stars. Some stars are bright and easy to see. Stars look small in the sky because they are trillions of miles away. But, some of these stars are actually bigger than the Sun. Other stars are smaller. The stars that are the farthest away are the hardest to see. You cannot see many stars without tools to help you.

Binoculars and **telescopes** are tools. You can use these tools to see stars better. These tools make stars that are far away look bigger. You can see more stars with a telescope than with just your eyes.

Telescopes might have tubes, mirrors, and lenses. These parts collect light. This helps to give a bigger and clearer view of objects in the sky. Scientists might use telescopes like this. They also use other kinds of telescopes that do not collect light. They collect other kinds of waves, such as radio waves.

Patterns of Stars

Did you ever see stars that are in groups or shapes? A group of stars that makes a pattern is a **constellation.** You can see the pattern if you imagine that lines are drawn between the stars. Look at the pictures on page 439 in your textbook. You can see the constellations called the Big Dipper and the Little Dipper.

People who lived a long time ago saw animals, people, and objects in star patterns. They made up stories about the constellations. They gave the constellations names. People who lived in Greece saw a constellation of a hunter. They named this constellation Orion. This name is still used today.

The stars in a constellation look like they are close together. But they are really very far apart.

We can see different patterns of stars at different times of the year. This is because Earth revolves around the Sun. The patterns of stars also change with Earth's four seasons. Like the Sun, stars do not move.

Lesson 4 Checkpoint

1. What are two tools that can help you see stars?

_____

_____

2. What do modern telescopes do?

_____

_____

3. What is a constellation?

_____

_____

Lesson 1: What are the parts of the solar system?

Vocabulary

planet a large body of matter that revolves, or travels, around the Sun

solar system the Sun, the nine planets and their moons, and other objects that revolve around the Sun

orbit the path an object takes as it revolves around the Sun

asteroids chunks of rock of different sizes that orbit the Sun

The Sun

The Sun is a star. It is made of hot, burning gases. The Sun looks larger and brighter than other stars because it is much closer to Earth. The Sun is very big. It is 100 times as wide as Earth. The Sun is so big that it could hold one million Earths inside it!

The temperature of the Sun's surface is 5,500°C. The center of the Sun is even hotter. The Sun's gravity packs hot gas particles together very tightly, and they join together. This gives the particles a lot of energy. The Sun gives off energy that moves in all directions. Some of the Sun's energy reaches Earth as sunlight.

How Objects in the Solar System Move

We live on the planet Earth. A **planet** is a large body of matter. Planets revolve around the Sun. The **solar system** is made of the Sun, nine planets, the planets' moons, and other objects that revolve around the Sun.

Look at pages 456–457 in your textbook. This picture shows each planet's **orbit.** An orbit is the oval-shaped path each planet takes as it revolves around the Sun. Planets that are closer to the Sun have shorter orbits. The strong pull of gravity holds the planets in their orbits.

The planets that are closer to the Sun are called the inner planets. These are Mercury, Venus, Earth, and Mars. Mercury is the planet closest to the Sun. It is about 58 million kilometers from the Sun. Outer planets are farther from the Sun. The five outer planets are Jupiter, Saturn, Uranus, Neptune, and Pluto. Pluto is the farthest planet from the Sun. It is usually about 6 billion kilometers from the Sun.

Asteroids are also part of the solar system. Asteroids are chunks of rock objects of different sizes. Asteroids orbit the Sun between the planets. Most asteroids are between Mars and Jupiter.

© Pearson Education, Inc. 3

Lesson 1 Checkpoint

1. Why is the Sun so bright and hot?

_____

_____

2. What makes up the solar system?

_____

_____

_____

3. How do objects in the solar system move?

_____

_____

Lesson 2: What are the planets?

The Inner Planets

Mercury, Venus, Earth, and Mars are the four inner planets. These planets are closer to the Sun than the outer planets. The inner planets are rocky. They do not have rings around them, and they do not have many moons.

The inner planets are of different sizes. Mercury, the second smallest planet, is dry, very hot, and has many craters. Venus, a little smaller than Earth, is also a very hot, rocky planet with craters, mountains, and valleys. Mars is the "Red Planet" because of its reddish-orange, rocky, dusty surface. It is half the size of Earth. Earth, the third planet from the Sun, is a little larger than Venus.

The inner planets rotate at different speeds. For example, it takes Earth 24 hours to rotate once. But it takes Venus 243 days to rotate.

The inner planets revolve around the Sun at different speeds. Mercury takes 88 days while Earth takes 365 days to travel around the Sun.

Earth Supports Life

Earth is very different from the other planets. It is the only planet that can support life. Earth has the mild temperatures, water, and atmosphere that living things need. Earth's atmosphere has the right amounts of oxygen and carbon dioxide. The atmosphere also protects us from the Sun's dangerous rays. Earth's gravity holds the atmosphere close to Earth.

Sunlight warms Earth and gives plants energy to grow. But not all of the Sun's light reaches Earth's surface. The atmosphere soaks up some of this light. Some light reflects off the ground and clouds. Gases in the atmosphere scatter this light. This makes the sky look blue.

Earth's rocky surface is made of sections called plates. These are on land and under the sea. These plates are always moving. Sometimes, they slide past each other. Sometimes plates bump into each other, causing earthquakes or volcanoes. The plates keep changing Earth's surface.

The Gas Giants

The five outer planets are Jupiter, Saturn, Uranus, Neptune, and Pluto. They are much farther apart than the inner planets. Most of the outer planets are huge and are called gas giants. This is because the outer planets are mostly made of gases. Jupiter and Saturn are the two largest gas giants. The outer planets are different from the inner planets in two other ways. The outer planets have rings around them. Also, most of these planets have many moons. Like the inner planets, most of the outer planets rotate at different speeds around the Sun.

Uranus, Neptune, and Pluto

Uranus and Neptune are about the same size. They are smaller than Saturn and Jupiter. But they are much bigger than the inner planets and Pluto. Pluto is the smallest planet in the solar system. It is the only outer planet that is not made of gas.

Is It a Planet?

In 2004, scientists discovered a tenth planet they called Sedna. It is much farther from the Sun than Pluto. Sedna is smaller than Pluto. Many scientists, however, do not think Sedna is a real planet. Scientists have found other small objects beyond Pluto. They call Sedna and these objects "planetoids."

Lesson 2 Checkpoint

1. Which of the nine planets are inner planets?

_____

_____

2. ◉ **Compare and Contrast** How do the sizes of the four inner planets compare?

_____

_____

_____

3. What makes life on Earth possible?

_____

_____

4. In what ways are Jupiter and Saturn alike?

_____

_____

5. Which of the nine planets are outer planets?

_____

_____

_____

6. Which of the outer planets is not a gas giant?

_____

7. ◉ **Compare and Contrast** On a two-column chart, list the ways that the inner planets and the gas giants are alike and different.

Lesson 1: How does technology affect our lives?

Vocabulary

tool an object used to do work

technology the use of knowledge to design new tools and new ways to do things

invention something made for the first time

Finding New Ways

People invent **tools** to help them do work more easily. A computer is a tool. Using tools helps people think of new ways of doing things. **Technology** is the use of knowledge to design new tools and new ways to do things.

The invention of arches was important technology in ancient Rome. An **invention** is something that is made for the first time. The Romans invented the arches to build bridges. Romans also used the arches to carry water from mountain springs to cities.

Technology in Your Home

Technologies in our homes work together as systems. For example, faucets, drains, and pipes work together as a plumbing system. You use the plumbing system when you take a bath. Some water in this system passes through a water heater. This is part of the electrical system. Electricity heats the water.

A home heating system also works with the electrical system. The furnace burns fuel for heat. But the heating system needs the electrical system to turn it on and off.

Technology Yesterday, Today, and Tomorrow

In the early 1800s, there was no electricity. A kitchen did not have a refrigerator to keep things cold. People had to burn wood in a stove to cook their food. It took all day to make a meal.

In time, new ways of storing food were invented. Ice boxes held ice to keep food cold. Later, electric refrigerators kept food cold.

Technology has changed kitchens in many ways. Now, microwaves cook food in a few minutes. Electric dishwashers wash dishes. Plastic bowls make it easy to store food.

Not long ago, music was stored and played on a record. The record had lines or grooves. A needle moved along these lines. The machine read the vibrations in the needle and translated the vibrations into music.

Now, we use CD players. A CD player has a light beam that reads and plays music that is stored on a disc.

How will technology affect our homes in the future? Some people think computers will run the home. Computer chips in each package of food will tell the oven how to cook it. The Internet will order food.

Lesson 1 Checkpoint

1. What is technology?

_____

_____

2. Explain how some technology systems work together in a house.

_____

_____

_____

_____

3. Why was the invention of the arch important technology in ancient Rome?

_____

_____

4. Explain the need for systems in order for technology to work in the home.

_____

_____

Lesson 2: What are some new technologies?

Vocabulary

> **computer** an electronic tool that stores, processes, and gets information

Tools for Extending Our Senses

Long ago, people on ships used math to find out where they were. Now people on ships use a Global Positioning System (GPS) to find out where they are. Satellites in space send the GPS signals. The GPS computer uses the signals to figure out the location and plan the route.

Some cars have GPS. Hikers also use GPS receivers to find their way in a forest. Farmers use GPS to locate the crops that need water, fertilizer, or pesticide. Satellite cameras can show which land areas are dry. Satellite cameras can show pictures of weather patterns too. Weather experts use these pictures to predict the weather.

Tools for Processing Information

A **computer** stores, processes, and sends electronic information very fast. For example, a computer can turn pieces of information about the weather into a weather forecast.

Computer technology is everywhere. Cameras, cars, calculators, and even watches have computer chips inside them.

Optical fibers are helping to make computers better. These fibers are thin wires of bendable glass that carry light. Optical fibers are in computers, telephones, and cable television systems. Optical fibers do not get hot as wires do. They also take up less space.

Tools for Transporting Materials

The National Highway System is a modern system of highways that goes from one state to another across the country. Millions of people use it to travel from one place to another. Trucks use the system to carry supplies to people all over the country.

Rivers made up the first transportation system in the United States. Today, boats are still used to carry freight. But today trains and planes also transport goods.

Unexpected Uses

Sometimes technology is useful in surprising ways. In 1946, Percy Spencer was testing a light bulb that used microwave energy. Microwaves are a kind of radiation.

One day, Spencer stood near the tube. A candy bar in his pocket melted. He put popcorn kernels near the microwave energy. They popped. This made Spencer think that microwaves might be able to cook other foods quickly. Today, many people use microwave ovens to cook food.

The first television sets and computers used glass tubes to display a picture. But these tubes could not be made for big screens because glass is heavy and breaks easily. In 1970, James Fergason invented a modern LCD screen. LCD stands for liquid crystal display. Liquid crystals glow when electricity hits them. This makes a picture on the screen. Liquid crystals are light and so the screens could be big. They are also flat.

© Pearson Education, Inc. 3

Lesson 2 Checkpoint

1. Explain how a GPS system helps people know where they are.

_____

_____

_____

2. Why is a modern roadway system important?

_____

_____

_____

3. What did Percy Spencer accidentally discover that microwaves could do?

_____

_____

4. What does a computer do?

_____

_____

Lesson 3: How does technology help us get energy?

Using Energy

Water and wind have been used as energy sources for centuries. Water mills were built next to rivers. A water mill has a big wheel. The force of the water turned the wheel. The wheel's energy was used to grind grain into flour.

Windmills were also used to do work. Windmills use the wind as a power source. They pumped water from under the ground.

There are good and bad things about using water mills and windmills. They do not pollute the air or water. But water mills only work along a river.

The energy of water is still used for some things. Water runs a modern lawn sprinkler. First, the hose sends water into the sprinkler. The pressure of the water makes the energy to do work. Then water turns a water wheel. The wheel turns some gears. The gears move the spray arm back and forth. The water in the spray arm waters the lawn.

Both wind and water are renewable energy sources. But they don't supply enough power for all our needs.

Producing Electricity

We still use water wheel technology inside hydroelectric power dams. Dams are built on rivers. The rivers back up behind the dams. This makes deep lakes. Gates open to let this water rush into the power station. The water's energy spins the water wheel in a generator. Water energy changes into electricity. This electricity is used for power in cities.

Hydroelectric power does not make much pollution. It is a renewable energy source. But, the lake behind the dam floods land. This changes the environment. Dams also affect fish.

Another way to change energy into electricity is by burning coal, oil, or natural gas. The burning fuel gives off heat. This heat is used to boil water. Boiling water makes steam. Pressure from steam turns wheels in electric generators. This makes electricity for everyone.

Burning fuel is also used to move cars. Cars get us from one place to another. But burning fuel can pollute the air. Pollution can be harmful to the environment. People are working on ways to make cars and generators that pollute less.

Future Sources of Energy

How will we meet our energy needs in the future? Solar energy is one answer. Solar energy comes from sunlight. It is a renewable energy source. Solar energy can be used to heat water. First, water runs through small tubes. Next, solar panels collect the Sun's rays. The sunlight is changed into heat. Then the heat warms the water in the tubes. Finally, the warm water flows into a tank. The water is stored until you need it.

Wind energy is another renewable energy source. Modern windmills have very big blades. Computer technology can tell when the wind changes direction. This technology can change the direction of the blades. The blades can keep catching the wind. Then the wind's energy can be changed into electricity.

Technology Timeline

The invention of the wheel and the Roman arches changed the way we get energy. The invention of satellites, airplanes, and telephones also improved our lives.

© Pearson Education, Inc. **3**

Lesson 3 Checkpoint

1. What renewable sources of energy have people used for centuries to generate power?

_____

2. 🎯 **Sequence** Use a graphic organizer and describe in steps how a modern water sprinkler works.

3. How are cars a helpful and a harmful example of technology?

_____

4. What two renewable energy resources might meet more of our energy needs in the future?

_____

_____

5. 🎯 **Sequence** List the steps that lead from the energy of sunshine in solar panels to the energy of hot water in a water tank. Use a graphic organizer.

6. What changes in technology have changed the way we get energy?

_____

_____

7. What must we do in order to continue to use nonrenewable fuel resources for energy?

_____

_____